Religion and Law in Ireland

Religion and Law in Ireland

Second Edition

Kathryn O'Sullivan

This book was originally published as a monograph in the International Encyclopaedia of Laws/Religion Law.

Founding Editor: Roger Blanpain
General Editor: Frank Hendrickx
Volume Editor: Wouter Druwé

Wolters Kluwer

Published by:
Kluwer Law International B.V.
PO Box 316
2400 AH Alphen aan den Rijn
The Netherlands
E-mail: lrs-sales@wolterskluwer.com
Website: www.wolterskluwer.com/en/solutions/kluwerlawinternational

Sold and distributed by:
Wolters Kluwer Legal & Regulatory U.S.
920 Links Avenue
Landisville, PA 17538
United States of America
E-mail: customer.service@wolterskluwer.com

ISBN 978-94-035-1728-5

e-Book: ISBN 978-94-035-1738-4
web-PDF: ISBN 978-94-035-1748-3

The Author

Dr Kathryn O'Sullivan is an Associate Professor of Law at the School of Law, University of Limerick, Ireland. Kathryn's research interests lie in family property law, succession law and law and religion in Ireland. She is the Corresponding Member for Ireland with the Cambridge Family Law Centre at the University of Cambridge and was selected as a Dobbin Atlantic Scholar for 2017–2018 by the Ireland Canada University Foundation. She has published widely in highly respected national and international journals (including *Legal Studies*, the *Journal of Family Studies* and the *International Journal of Law, Policy and the Family*) and was the sole editor of *Minority Religions under Irish Law: Islam in National and International Context* published by Brill in 2019. In terms of impact, she has provided expert evidence to the Women and Equalities Committee of the UK Parliament on the issue of cohabitants' rights and her work has been cited in the British Columbia Court of Appeal in Canada as well as by the Law Reform Commission of Ireland.

The Author

Table of Contents

Table of Contents

List of Abbreviations

AC	Appeals Cases (England and Wales)
ALL ER	All England Law Reports
AMRI	Association of Leaders of Missionaries and Religious of Ireland
ASAI	Advertising Standards Authority for Ireland
BAI	Broadcasting Authority of Ireland
DCIF	Dublin City Interfaith Forum
DPP	Director of Public Prosecutions
ECHR	European Convention on Human Rights
ECtHR	European Court of Human Rights
EEA	European Economic Area
EU	European Union
GDPR	General Data Protection Regulation
ICCI	Islamic Cultural Centre of Ireland
ICCL	Irish Council for Civil Liberties
ICCPR	International Covenant on Civil and Political Rights 1966
ICESCR	International Covenant on Economic, Social and Cultural Rights 1966
IEHC	Irish High Court
IESC	Irish Supreme Court
IFCO	Irish Film Classification Office
IHREC	Irish Human Rights and Equality Commission
ILRM	Irish Law Reports Monthly
ILTR	Irish Law Times Reports
IPRT	Irish Penal Reform Trust
IR	Irish Reports
MRF	Marriage Registration Form
PRSI	Pay Related Social Insurance
RTÉ	*Raidió Teilifís Éireann*
SI	Statutory Instrument

List of Abbreviations

TD	*Teachta Dála*
UDHR	Universal Declaration of Human Rights
UN	United Nations
WRC	Workplace Relations Commission

General Introduction

§1. General Background of the Country

1. The island of Ireland lies in the North West Atlantic Ocean and has been divided into two jurisdictions since 1922. To the south of the island lies the Republic of Ireland. To the north lies Northern Ireland, which is a part of the UK. This monograph relates exclusively to the Republic of Ireland.

2. As of April 2022, the population of the Republic of Ireland is approximately 5.15 million people. This figure has increased by over 2.3 million people over the past sixty years, rising from just over 2.8 million in 1961.[1] Notwithstanding that for centuries, Ireland was characterised by high levels of emigration to the UK and the United States of America in particular, inward migration has played an increasingly important role in Irish society over the past thirty years.[2] Ireland is divided into four provinces: Munster, Leinster, Connaught and Ulster. Although the population of all provinces has increased in recent decades, this increase has not been shared equally across all regions in Ireland. The capital of Ireland, Dublin, is located on the east coast of the province of Leinster. Growth in this region continues to outstrip all other regions. Leinster is now home to over half of the total population, with almost 1.5 million people residing in Dublin city and county alone.[3]

3. From a political perspective, Ireland is regarded as a constitutional republic with a parliamentary system of government. A bicameral national parliament, known as Oireachtas Éireann, is comprised of the President of Ireland (also known as Uachtarán na hÉireann) and the two houses of the Oireachtas: Seanad Éireann (Senate) and Dáil Éireann (House of Representatives). The official residence of the President of Ireland is called Áras an Uachtaráin, and the houses of the Oireachtas

1. Central Statistics Office, *Census 2022 Summary Results* (2023) available at https://www.cso.ie/en/releasesandpublications/ep/p-cpsr/censusofpopulation2022-summaryresults/populationchanges/ (accessed 8 Jun. 2023).
2. Central Statistics Office, *Census 2016 Summary Results: Part 1,* 10 (2017) available at, https://www.cso.ie/en/media/csoie/newsevents/documents/census2016summaryresultspart1/Census2016SummaryPart1.pdf (accessed 26 Aug. 2019). Reflecting on the fluctuations in migration to and from Ireland, the Central Statistics Office note that of the three factors that determine population change (births, deaths and net migration), results suggest that 'from an Irish perspective net migration is by far the most influential, volatile and uncertain'.
3. Central Statistics Office, *Press Statement Census of Population 2022 – Summary Results Dublin* (2023) available at, https://www.cso.ie/en/csolatestnews/pressreleases/2023pressreleases/pressstatementcensusofpopulation2022-summaryresultsdublin/ (accessed 8 Jun. 2023).

meet at Leinster House on Dublin's Kildare Street. The Taoiseach (Prime Minister) acts as the head of the government and is appointed by the President upon the nomination of the Dáil. The Dáil itself is comprised of 158 members known as TDs or Teachtaí Dála (Members of Parliament). TDs are elected pursuant to a system of proportional representation (with a single transferable vote) to represent multi-seat constituencies. The Seanad, meanwhile, is composed of sixty members or senators. Eleven senators are nominated by the Taoiseach, six are elected by university graduates, and forty-three are elected by public representatives from panels of candidates established on a vocational basis.

§2. Social Facts about Religion

4. Ireland remains a predominantly Roman Catholic country. In 2022, 69% of the population continued to be identified as Catholic, albeit this figure was down significantly from just a decade earlier when, in 2011, 84.2% of the population was so identified.[4] Other Christian churches, including the Church of Ireland, Presbyterian and Apostolic or Pentecostal Churches, have also witnessed declines. This decline for Christian religions has been counterbalanced by a significant rise in the number of respondents who identified as having 'no religion'. This cohort grew by 272% from 269,800 in 2011 to 736,210 in 2022.[5] Consequently, those with no religion now account for approximately 14% of the population.

5. However, the trends are not all towards an increase in secularisation. Various non-Christian religions, particularly Orthodox, Hindu and Muslim communities, have seen significant increases since 2011. The Orthodox Church now represents the third-largest religion in the State with over 100,000 followers[6] while Ireland's Muslim community has also grown dramatically in recent years. While only 3,875 persons were recorded as Muslim in the 1991 census, this figure rose to 19,147 in 2002, 32,539 in 2006 and 49,204 in 2011.[7] The latest official census recorded almost

4. Central Statistics Office, *Census of Population 2022 – Summary Results* (2023) available at https://www.cso.ie/en/releasesandpublications/ep/p-cpsr/censusofpopulation2022-summaryresults/migrationanddiversity/ (accessed 8 Jun. 2023); Central Statistics Office, *Census 2016 Summary Results: Part 1*, 72 (2017) available at, https://www.cso.ie/en/media/csoie/newsevents/documents/census2016summaryresultspart1/Census2016SummaryPart1.pdf (accessed 26 Aug. 2019).
5. Central Statistics Office, Census of Population 2022 – Summary Results (2023) available at, https://www.cso.ie/en/releasesandpublications/ep/p-cpsr/censusofpopulation2022-summaryresults/migrationanddiversity/ (accessed 8 Jun. 2023); Central Statistics Office, *Census 2016 Summary Results: Part 1*, 72 (2017) available at https://www.cso.ie/en/media/csoie/newsevents/documents/census2016summaryresultspart1/Census2016SummaryPart1.pdf (accessed 26 Aug. 2019).
6. Central Statistics Office, *Census of Population 2022 – Summary Results* (2023) available at https://www.cso.ie/en/releasesandpublications/ep/p-cpsr/censusofpopulation2022-summaryresults/migrationanddiversity/ (accessed 8 Jun. 2023).
7. Central Statistics Office, *Census 2011 Profile 7: Religion Ethnicity and Irish Travellers*, 16 (Dublin: Stationery Office, 2012).

82,000 Muslims in Ireland in 2022, representing 1.5% of the population or quadruple the 2002 figures reported twenty years earlier.[8] Moreover, the community is quite young in relation to the wider population. The average age of Muslims in 2016 was 26.0 years,[9] with 10,884 children of primary school-going age (5–12-year-olds) and 5,480 of secondary school-going age (13–18-year-olds).[10] Considerable academic attention has also fallen on the diversity of Muslim migration to Ireland with Scharbrodt noting the lack of any particularly dominant ethnic or cultural group.[11]

6. One way in which, perhaps, a more accurate picture of the overall religious landscape in Ireland can be obtained is through a consideration of the changes which have been evidenced over the past thirty years in the ways in which wedding ceremonies are celebrated in the jurisdiction.[12] Reflecting the socio-religious norms of the time, 96.5% of all weddings conducted in Ireland in 1987 were religious wedding ceremonies, with 93.3% of all weddings conducted according to Roman Catholic rites alone.[13] In the intervening years, however (and cognisant that divorce was only introduced into the jurisdiction in 1996),[14] wedding practice has undergone profound change. In 2007, 74% of all weddings conducted in the State were Roman Catholic ceremonies,[15] while by 2017, this figure had fallen to 50.9%.[16] Figures for 2022 show another dramatic decline, with just 40% of weddings conducted recorded as Roman Catholic ceremonies.[17] Weddings conducted according to the rites of the Church of Ireland have also witnessed a steady drop in recent decades.[18] Religious denominations other than the Roman Catholic Church, the Church of Ireland or the

8. Central Statistics Office, *Census of Population 2022 – Summary Results* (2023) available at https://www.cso.ie/en/releasesandpublications/ep/p-cpsr/censusofpopulation2022-summaryresults/migrationanddiversity/ (accessed 8 Jun. 2023).
9. The State average is 37.4 years: Central Statistics Office, *Census of Population 2016 – Profile 8 Irish Travellers, Ethnicity and Religion* available at http://www.cso.ie/en/releasesandpublications/ep/p-cp8iter/p8iter/p8rnc/ (accessed 26 Aug. 2019).
10. Central Statistics Office, *Census of Population 2016: Profile 8 Irish Travellers, Ethnicity and Religion* available at http://www.cso.ie/en/releasesandpublications/ep/p-cp8iter/p8iter/p8rnc/ (accessed 26 Aug. 2019). Unfortunately, results of Census 2022 regarding the age profile for the Muslim community are not available at the time of writing.
11. Oliver Scharbrodt, 'Muslim Immigration to the Republic of Ireland: Trajectories and Dynamics since World War II' 47(1) *Éire-Ireland* 221, 231 (2012). *See also* Oliver Scharbrodt et al. (eds), *Muslims in Ireland: Past and Present* 49–72 (Edinburgh University Press, 2015).
12. Note, marriage remains popular in Ireland. According to the Central Statistics Office of Ireland, in 2022, 23,173 marriages were registered in the jurisdiction. Central Statistics Office, *Marriage 2022* available at https://www.cso.ie/en/releasesandpublications/ep/p-mar/marriages2022/mainresults/ (accessed 8 Jun. 2023). Of these, there were 619 same-sex marriages.
13. Central Statistics Office, *Report on Vital Statistics 1987,* 258 (Stationery Office, 1990).
14. *See* Part X for more.
15. Central Statistics Office, *Marriages 2007* available at http://www.cso.ie/en/media/csoie/releasespublications/documents/vitalstats/2007/marriages2007.pdf (accessed 3 Apr. 2018).
16. Central Statistics Office, *Marriages 2017* available at http://www.cso.ie/en/releasesandpublications/er/mar/marriages2017/ (accessed 3 Apr. 2018). Note, in 2017, 63% of all weddings were religious.
17. Central Statistics Office, *Marriage 2022* available at https://www.cso.ie/en/releasesandpublications/ep/p-mar/marriages2022/mainresults/ (accessed 8 Jun. 2023).
18. Central Statistics Office, *Marriage 2022* available at https://www.cso.ie/en/releasesandpublications/ep/p-mar/marriages2022/mainresults/ (accessed 8 Jun. 2023).

Presbyterian Church, by contrast, have seen a (sometimes significant) growth in their marriage rates. Of particular note, in this regard, is the year-on-year increase seen in the number of weddings conducted by the Spiritualist Union of Ireland since first reported in 2014. Spiritualist weddings in 2022, for example, accounted for almost 10% of all wedding ceremonies,[19] albeit it is important to remember that neither of the intending spouses is required to be a Spiritualist nor to be a member of the Spiritualist Union of Ireland to choose such a ceremony. Indeed, although there appears to be no data on the precise number of Spiritualists in Ireland, anecdotal evidence would suggest that a significant proportion of those marrying in Spiritualist ceremonies would not self-describe as Spiritualists. Wedding ceremonies conducted by 'other religions', that is to say, those other than Roman Catholic, Church of Ireland, Presbyterian and Spiritualist ceremonies, have also seen a sharp growth in recent times.[20]

7. While these figures are undoubtedly demonstrative of the greater religious diversity in an increasingly multicultural Ireland, there has also been a distinct increase in more secular belief systems. In particular, since the introduction of the Civil Registration (Amendment) Act 2012, facilitating the legal recognition of secular weddings in Ireland, weddings conducted by the Humanist Association of Ireland have grown dramatically and represented 7.8% of marriages conducted in 2017.[21] In the interim, this figure has risen even further, with secular weddings accounting for 9.3% of all weddings conducted in Ireland in 2022.[22] Finally, just over a quarter of all marriage ceremonies in Ireland involve civil marriages. This figure has remained largely constant in recent years.[23]

8. It is clear, therefore, that there has been a significant social change with regard to individuals' preferences for marriage solemnisation, which is likely indicative of changes in religious beliefs in Ireland over recent decades. Although the decline in weddings conducted according to the rites of the Roman Catholic Church would appear to speak to some degree of abandonment of traditional Irish socio-religious norms, it is interesting that the shifts have not been towards civil ceremonies per se but often in the direction of alternative religious or secular organisations such as the

---

19. Central Statistics Office, *Marriage 2022* available at https://www.cso.ie/en/releasesandpublications/ep/p-mar/marriages2022/mainresults/ (accessed 8 Jun. 2023).
20. These weddings accounted for 5.1% of all wedding ceremonies in 2017, Central Statistics Office, *Marriages 2007* available at http://www.cso.ie/en/releasesandpublications/er/mar/marriages2017/ (accessed 3 Apr. 2018). In 2022, however, 'other religions' accounted for 12.9% of all wedding ceremonies conducted, *see* Central Statistics Office, *Marriage 2022* available at https://www.cso.ie/en/releasesandpublications/ep/p-mar/marriages2022/mainresults/ (accessed 8 Jun. 2023). For more on these trends in general, *see* Susan Leahy & Kathryn O'Sullivan, 'Changing Conceptions of Marriage in Ireland: Law and Practice' 30(3) *Child and Family Law Quarterly* 279 (2018).
21. Central Statistics Office, *Marriages 2017* available at http://www.cso.ie/en/releasesandpublications/er/mar/marriages2017/ (accessed 3 Apr. 2018). Although the CSO describe these weddings as 'Humanist' as opposed to 'secular', non-Humanist secular weddings may also be conducted.
22. Central Statistics Office, *Marriage 2022* available at https://www.cso.ie/en/releasesandpublications/ep/p-mar/marriages2022/mainresults/ (accessed 8 Jun. 2023).
23. In 2022, civil ceremonies accounted for 26.2% of all weddings conducted, *see* Central Statistics Office, *Marriage 2022* available at https://www.cso.ie/en/releasesandpublications/ep/p-mar/marriages2022/mainresults/ (accessed 8 Jun. 2023).

Spiritualist Union of Ireland and the Humanist Association of Ireland, respectively, which now conduct approximately one in five wedding ceremonies celebrated in Ireland annually.

§3. Historical Background

9. Christianity first arrived in Ireland in approximately the fifth century AD. Influenced in no small part by the arrival of Saint Patrick, it soon spread across the country, with early Christian Ireland identified by its many monastic settlements. Throughout the ninth and tenth centuries, these monasteries became a target for the invading Vikings. Settlements were destroyed, sacred relics were stolen, and religious ministers were murdered. Nevertheless, during this period, 'a sophisticated indigenous system of law' known as Brehon Law prevailed under which 'an important place was reserved for the early Christian Church'.[24] As Bacik explains: 'Triad 200 sums up Brehon governance as comprising: "the three rocks to which lawful behaviour is tied: monastery, lord, kin".'[25]

10. The arrival of Anglo-Norman forces in the twelfth century saw the steady decline of Brehon Law[26] while the position of Catholicism in Ireland came under ever-increasing pressure, in particular, from the sixteenth century. The English Reformation saw the Church of England break away from the Roman Catholic Church while at the same time Henry VIII placed an even greater focus on bringing Ireland under a much tighter rule. During the subsequent Tudor conquest of Ireland in the sixteenth and seventeenth centuries, religious identification gained ever-increasing prominence, with the Catholic Irish subject to religious discrimination and persecution. Land was confiscated from Catholic Irish landowners and resettled in favour of Protestant English and Scottish colonists.[27] The brutal Penal Laws were also introduced as a means of forcing Irish Catholics (and Protestant dissenters) to be subject to the British Crown and accepting the established Church of Ireland. However, despite the emergence of a Protestant ascendancy after the Williamite wars and the continued imposition of the Penal Laws until the late eighteenth century, the Irish remained overwhelmingly Catholic.[28] It has been noted:

> Particularly in the late eighteenth century, the drastic restrictions imposed upon the rights of Catholics merely strengthened the Church's position in society,

---

24. Ivana Bacik, 'Future Directions for the Constitution' in Eoin Carolan & Oran Doyle (eds) *The Irish Constitution: Governance and Values* 135, 139 (Roundhall, 2008).
25. Ivana Bacik, 'Future Directions for the Constitution' in Eoin Carolan & Oran Doyle (eds) *The Irish Constitution: Governance and Values* 135, 139 (Roundhall, 2008).
26. For more *see* Art Cosgrove (ed.), *A New History of Ireland: Medieval Ireland 1169–1534* (Vol. 2) (OUP, 2008).
27. For more, *see* Theodore William Moody, Francis Xavier Martin & Francis John Byrne (eds), *A New History of Ireland: Early Modern Ireland, 1534–1691* (Vol. 3) (OUP, 2009).
28. For more, *see* Theodore William Moody & William E. Vaughan (eds), *A New History of Ireland: Eighteenth Century Ireland 1691–1800* (Vol. 4) (OUP, 2009).

> and the will of the people to practice their chosen faith. Catholicism thus became the religion of social and political defiance, of nationhood and patriotic identity … .[29]

11. The situation improved for Irish Catholics with Catholic emancipation in the early nineteenth century and the removal of much of the statutory discrimination against Catholics. Although religion continued to be an issue of contention, with the vast majority of Irish land still held by Protestant (often absentee) landlords,[30] the Roman Catholic Church 'amassed significant power, gaining ownership and control over many schools, hospitals and social services across Ireland'.[31]

12. The War of Independence from 1919 to 1921 resulted in the partition of Ireland, with independence from Britain secured for twenty-six of the thirty-two counties on the island. In the predominantly Roman Catholic and nationalist Irish Free State to the south (subsequently declared a republic in 1949), the Catholic Church 'moved into alignment with those in power in the new Free State, making its influence felt in every sphere of public life'.[32]

13. While independence brought peace south of the border (albeit after a civil war), religious tensions continued to give rise to conflict between Catholics and Protestants in British-controlled, unionist-majority Northern Ireland, particularly from the late-1960s. The Northern Ireland peace process resulted in the Belfast/Good Friday Agreement in 1998 which brought an end to 'The Troubles'.[33] Given this backdrop, it has been observed that:

> concerns as to the role of religion in public life [in Ireland] are linked to a distinct historical context, in which religious differences have formed the backdrop to an independence struggle, violent conflict and fragile peace negotiations.[34]

---

29. Ivana Bacik, 'Future Directions for the Constitution' in Eoin Carolan & Oran Doyle (eds) *The Irish Constitution: Governance and Values* 135, 139 (Roundhall, 2008).
30. For more, *see* William E. Vaughan (ed.), *A New History of Ireland: Ireland under the Union, I: 1801–1870* (Vol. 5) (OUP, 2009) and William E. Vaughan (ed.), *A New History of Ireland: Ireland under the Union, II: 1870–1921* (Vol. 6) (OUP, 2010).
31. Ivana Bacik, 'Future Directions for the Constitution' in Eoin Carolan & Oran Doyle (eds) *The Irish Constitution: Governance and Values* 135, 139 (Roundhall, 2008).
32. Ivana Bacik, 'Future Directions for the Constitution' in Eoin Carolan & Oran Doyle (eds) *The Irish Constitution: Governance and Values* 135, 139 (Roundhall, 2008). *See also* Gerard W. Hogan, 'Law and Religion: Church-State Relations in Ireland from Independence to the Present Day' 35(1) *The American Journal of Comparative Law* 47–96 (1987).
33. *See* Diarmaid Ferriter, *The Border: The Legacy of a Century of Anglo-Irish Politics* (Profile Books, 2019).
34. Siobhan Mullally & Darren O'Donovan, 'Religion in Ireland's "Public Squares": Education, the Family and Expanding Equality Claims' (April) *Public Law* 284, 285 (2011).

Part I. Legal Framework and Sources

Chapter 1. Constitutional Position of Religion

14. Following the declaration of Irish independence in 1922, the Constitution of the Irish Free State was first adopted. The second (and current) Irish Constitution, Bunreacht na hÉireann, was subsequently introduced in 1937. Although it has been described as 'inimical to the idea of a secular republic, and arguably of questionable propriety in an increasingly diverse society',[35] religion, in particular, receives high priority and the 'exalted position' it is afforded in the constitutional order has been recognised.[36]

15. Throughout, the Irish Constitution contains many references, both direct and indirect, which suggest the existence of a Christian, if not Catholic, state. The Preamble to the Constitution recognises the Tridentine God, while Article 6.1 of the Constitution states:

> All powers of government, legislative, executive and judicial, derive, under God, from the people, whose right it is to designate the rulers of the State and, in final appeal, to decide all questions of national policy, according to the requirements of the common good.

16. Reflecting this focus, various oaths for the office of President,[37] for membership of the Council of State[38] and membership of the Irish judiciary[39] also include references to 'the presence of Almighty God'.

---

35. Jamie McLoughlin, '"In the Presence of Almighty God": The Human Rights Violations at the Heart of the Irish Constitution' 35(17) *Irish Law Times* 230 (2017).
36. Eoin Daly, *Religion, Law and the Irish State* 82 (Clarus Press, 2012). Note, however, 'religion' is not defined within the Irish Constitution, *see* Gerard Whyte, 'On the Meaning of "Religion" under the Irish Constitution' in Eoin Carolan & Oran Doyle (eds) *The Irish Constitution: Governance and Values* 446 (Roundhall, 2008). Whyte noted at 460: 'To date, the issue of a legal definition of "religion" for either constitutional or statutory purposes has not arisen in the Irish courts. However, the recent growth in religious and cultural diversification in our society increases the possibility that some Irish judge will eventually have to resolve this question in relation to a belief system that is not explicitly listed or alluded to in constitutional and legislative texts.' For more *see* Part II Ch. 3. For a consideration of the role of religion under the Constitution of the Irish Free State, *see* Thomas Mohr, 'Religious Minorities under the Constitution of the Irish Free State, 1922–1937' (June 2021) 61(2) *American Journal of Legal History*, 235–272.
37. Article 12.8. Note, in *Shortall and Others v. Ireland* (2021) ECHR 349 (application no. 50272/18), the ECtHR considered a claim that the religious language contained in the declarations required

17. However, while these references to Christianity undoubtedly speak to the religious orientation of the overwhelming majority of the population in the early to mid-twentieth century (and hold undoubted symbolic value), it is nonetheless considered that the references are of non-legal power.[40] As Daly explains: 'At a minimum, it is well established that references to Christianity in the Constitution in no way condition or limit the scope of the religious freedom guarantees' carried elsewhere in the constitutional text.[41] Indeed, notwithstanding the religious rhetoric which permeates it, the 1937 Constitution actually vests 'all sovereign authority in temporal, public institutions, and for the most part, at least, [recognises] religion in a symbolic sense only'.[42]

18. Perhaps surprisingly, given the rhetoric outlined above, minimal formal legal privilege is extended to religions within the Constitution as a whole. While Roman Catholic teaching, in particular, has profoundly influenced various aspects of Irish law, as Daly explains, this influence was 'secured informally through the obeisance of legislators, abdicating in practice their constitutionally supreme position, in a sometimes supine acceptance of a duty to legislate in accordance with Catholic imperatives, as interpreted by the Irish hierarchy'.[43]

19. Article 44 represents the most important constitutional provision in respect of religion and is considered to signal a strong constitutional endorsement of the

under the Irish Constitution for the office of President of Ireland (Uachtarán na hÉireann) and for members of the Council of State breached the applicants' freedom of conscience and freedom of religion. The Court unanimously declared the application inadmissible holding that the applicants had not provided reasonable and convincing evidence that they were at risk of being directly affected by these requirements and thus were not able to claim to be victims of a violation of the Convention.

38. Article 31.4.
39. Article 34.6.1.
40. *See* GW Hogan, 'Legal Aspects of Church/State Relations In Ireland' (1988) 7 *St. Louis University Public Law Review* 275; Gerard Whyte, 'Religion and the Irish Constitution', (1996–1997) 30 *John Marshall Law Review* 725.
41. Eoin Daly, *Religion, Law and the Irish State* 116 (Clarus Press, 2012). Referring to the Preamble and Art. 6, Jamie McLoughlin, '"In the Presence of Almighty God": The Human Rights Violations at the Heart of the Irish Constitution' 35(17) *Irish Law Times* 230 (2017) notes these 'and various other references to the Christian (and specifically Catholic) religion in the Constitution are … relatively innocuous'. He raised concerns, however, regarding the prohibition on blasphemy as originally applied under Art. 40.6.1° and, as noted above, the oaths required of various office holders under the constitution. *See also* John Kelly, 'The Constitution: Law and Manifesto' in Frank Litton (ed.) *The Constitution of Ireland 1937–1987,* 208 (Institute of Public Administration, 1988).
42. Eoin Daly, *Religion, Law and the Irish State* 5–6 (Clarus Press, 2012).
43. Eoin Daly, *Religion, Law and the Irish State* 3–4 (Clarus Press, 2012). It is important to also note that Art. 44 has been subject to constitutional reform. In its original format, Art. 44 referred to the 'special position of the Holy Catholic Apostolic and Roman Church as the guardian of the Faith professed by the great majority of the citizens' and 'recognised' minority denominations including the Church of Ireland, the Presbyterian Church in Ireland, the Methodist Church in Ireland, the Religious Society of Friends in Ireland, the Jewish Congregations as well as 'the other religious denominations existing' in Ireland in 1937. Notwithstanding that the reference to the 'special position' of the Catholic Church was also not considered to have legal effect (as acknowledged, albeit obiter, by Geoghegan J in *Ó Beoláin v. Fahy* [2001] 2 IR 279), following the Fifth Amendment to the Constitution in Ireland in 1972, this reference was removed. *See* Part II Ch. 3 for more.

freedom of religion. Pursuant to Article 44.2.1°, the Constitution guarantees 'Freedom of conscience and the free profession and practice of religion' for every citizen, subject only to 'public order and morality'. Moreover, Article 44.2.3° confirms that 'The State shall not impose any disabilities or make any discrimination on the ground of religious profession, belief or status.' Article 44.2.2° prohibits any state endowment of religion, while denominational autonomy for religions is protected by Article 44.2.5°.

20. A general equality guarantee for citizens is also carried out in Article 40.1 of the Irish Constitution. It provides that 'All citizens shall, as human persons, be held equal before the law.' However, important caveats are included as it further notes: 'This shall not be held to mean that the State shall not in its enactments have due regard to differences of capacity, physical and moral, and of social function.'[44]

44. For more, *see* Part VII Ch. 7.

Chapter 2. Other Legislation with Regard to Religion

21. In the absence of well-developed statutory law relating to religion, the Constitution has been identified as 'the most significant legal instrument regulating the State-religion relationship, in practical as well as formal terms'.[45] Despite this, however, various pieces of legislation impacting religion and religious communities will be addressed throughout this monograph. The legal status of religious communities will be considered in Part III, while important legislation pertaining to issues of education and family law will be dealt with in Parts IX and X, respectively. Legislation pertaining to protections of the individual, labour law, criminal law and non-discrimination are also addressed throughout the monograph.

45. Eoin Daly, *Religion, Law and the Irish State* 20 (Clarus Press, 2012).

Chapter 3. Typology of the System

22. European countries are characterised by three primary models of Church-State relations: so-called State Church Systems, Separation (Secular) Systems and Cooperationist (Hybrid) Systems.[46] Despite the rhetoric of the Irish Constitution, and perhaps contrary to popular perception, Ireland, like France and the Netherlands, applies a 'Separation System'.[47] It is well established that religion has only ever represented an indirect source of legal authority in Ireland with no established church in the jurisdiction: religions are thus legally 'private'.[48] Moreover, as will be discussed in Part VIII, there is a constitutional barrier forbidding the endowment of any religion in Ireland.

---

46. Russell Sandberg, 'Church-State Relations in Europe: From Legal Models to an Interdisciplinary Approach' 1(3) *Journal of Religion in Europe* 329–352 (2008).
47. Gerard Hogan preface to Dermot Keogh & Andrew McCarthy, *The Making of the 1937 Constitution* 17 (Mercer, 2007) observed that the removal of the provision originally carried in Art. 44 which referred to the 'special position' of the Roman Catholic Church and recognised various other churches allowed the 'secular nature' of the Constitution to come to the fore.
48. *See* Part III for more.

Part II. Religious Freedom in General

Introduction

23. Religious freedom, whether individual or collective, is reflected in various sources of law, including constitutional law, international human rights law and common law. Very often, provisions relating to religious freedoms are characterised as individual rights, albeit that they may be enjoyed by many within and across various religious groups, individually or together. As a result, it has been observed that there is often no meaningful distinction between individual and collective religious freedoms.[49]

24. Certain religious groups have, however, long enjoyed special, denominationally specific protections under Irish law and policy. Pursuant to section 15 of the Slaughter of Animals Act 1935, notwithstanding rules regarding the compulsory use of approved instruments for the slaughter of animals, Jewish and Muslim slaughter methods were permitted.[50] More recently, the latest policy document on the Uniform and Dress Code within An Garda Síochána, the Irish police force, provides that, notwithstanding the general ban on the wearing of symbols and adornments, headwear for religious and cultural reasons and beliefs, for example, the Sikh turban and the Muslim hijab, will be supported 'where possible'.[51][52]

25. Yet, notwithstanding these limited examples, legislation seeking to protect religious individuals or groups in Ireland is almost exclusively framed in denominationally neutral terms. Although the Burial Ground (Amendment) Regulations 2013 were introduced to permit shroud burial practices in response to calls from the

49. For a general discussion of how the law may protect religion as both an individual and a collective right, albeit in the context of England and Wales, *see* Russell Sandberg, 'Religion and the Individual: A Socio-Legal Perspective' in Abby Day (ed.) *Religion and the Individual* 157–168 (Ashgate, 2008).

50. For modern legislation in this regard, *see* the Animal, Health and Welfare Act 2013. *See also* European Union (Protection of Animals at the Time of Killing) Regulations 2013.

51. Policy Document (2021) p. 9 at https://www.garda.ie/en/about-us/publications/policy-documents/uniform-and-dress-code-within-an-garda-siochana-policy.pdf (accessed 6 Nov. 2023). The pressure to make such a change was evident in the case of *Ravinder Singh Oberoi v. Commissioner of An Garda Síochána* [2013] IEHC 267; [2014] 25 ELR 17 *see* Part VII Ch. 7 §3 below.

52. Paul Reynolds, 'Gardaí to Permit Wearing of Turbans and Hijabs in Diversity Drive' (RTÉ, 4 Apr. 2019) available at https://www.rte.ie/news/2019/0404/1040561-garda_recruitment/ (accessed 24 Jul. 2019). *See also* Sorcha Pollak, 'Badge of distinction: Meet the first Sikh in the Garda Reserves' (*Irish Times*, 23 Jan. 2021). *See* further, Part VII, Ch. 7.

Muslim community, the amendments made to the Rules and Regulations for the Regulation of Burial Grounds 1888 permit 'uncoffined burials', with no reference to shrouds or Islamic traditions.[53] 'Ministers of religion', moreover, are exempt from jury service pursuant to the Juries Act 1976. Under section 9 of the Health Act 2007 (Care and Welfare of Residents In Designated Centres For Older People) Regulations 2013 (SI 415/2013), registered providers of nursing home care are required in their operations to have due regard to a number of features of their residents including their religious persuasion, racial origin and cultural and linguistic background. They are required to facilitate, insofar as is reasonably practicable, the exercise of residents' 'civil, political and religious rights'.[54] Likewise, the Prison Rules 2007 provide a section dedicated to the 'religious, spiritual and moral life' of prisoners and expressly provides for the provision of facilities for religious practice, generally. As will be discussed in Part VII Chapter 7, significant (non-denominational) protection against discrimination on the grounds of religion also exists in relation to the provision of goods and services as well as in relation to employment pursuant to the Equal Status Act 2000 (as amended) and the Employment Equality Act 1998 (as amended) respectively.

26. While there are, therefore, many elements to the ways in which Irish law facilitates religious freedom,[55] this part will place its focus on the freedom of religion provisions found in the Irish Constitution.[56]

53. Consequently, unless a direction has been issued not to do so on the grounds of there being a health or environmental risk, Muslim shroud burials are now permitted under Irish law.
54. Regulation 9(3)(e). *See* Part IX Ch. 3 for more.
55. *See* Gerard Whyte, 'On the Meaning of "Religion" under the Irish Constitution' in Eoin Carolan & Oran Doyle (eds) *The Irish Constitution: Governance and Values* 446, 448–449 note 9 (Roundhall, 2008) for other current and historical examples.
56. For Art. 9 of the ECHR and its implementation in Ireland, *see* Part IV Ch. 2.

Chapter 1. Individual Religious Freedom

27. The 'infamous historical influence of Catholic thought on legislation' in Ireland[57] and the 'influence of religion, and specifically the Catholic religion, on the making of the Constitution of 1937'[58] have long been recognised.[59] However, notwithstanding these influences, the Irish Constitution remains ostensibly neutral between religions, with significant importance having been attached to the need to guarantee denominational neutrality and religious freedom in the initial drafting of the Constitution of the Irish Free State in 1922 and, subsequently, in the drafting of the Second Constitution of Ireland, Bunreacht na hÉireann, in 1937.[60]

28. As noted in Part I Chapter 1, Article 44 is regarded as signalling a strong constitutional endorsement of the freedom of religion.[61] Pursuant to Article 44.2.1°, the Constitution guarantees freedom of conscience and the free profession and practice of religion for every citizen, subject only to 'public order and morality'.[62] Moreover, Article 44.2.3° confirms that the State shall not 'impose any disabilities or make any discrimination on the ground of religious profession, belief or status'.[63] The Constitution ensures equality in the funding of religious schools and furthermore recognises the right of non-coreligionist pupils to opt out of religious instruction in

57. Eoin Daly, *Religion, Law and the Irish State* 5 (Clarus, 2012).
58. Patrick Hannon, 'In God's Name, What Next? Religion, the Constitution and the New Ireland' in Eoin Carolan & Oran Doyle (eds) *The Irish Constitution: Governance and Values* 463, 463 (Roundhall, 2008). Eoin Daly, 'Accommodating Religious Minorities in Ireland: The Constitutional Framework' in Kathryn O'Sullivan (ed.) *Minority Religions under Irish Law: Islam in National and International Context* 34, 35 (Brill, 2019) also notes 'certain bellicose, even triumphalist provisions' in the Irish Constitution which 'place religion in general, and even Christian religions specifically, at the centre of public identity'.
59. *See* Siobhan Mullally & Darren O'Donovan, 'Religion and Ireland's "Public Squares": Education, the Family and Expanding Equality Claims' (April) *Public Law* 284, 284 (2011) who note 'Although the 1937 Constitution … did not provide for any established Church, and explicitly protected religious freedom, a conservative Catholic ethos permeated much of the constitutional text. The implicit contract between the Catholic Church and the State both shaped and constrained the development of fundamental rights jurisprudence for many years.'
60. Eoin Daly, 'Accommodating Religious Minorities in Ireland: The Constitutional Framework' in Kathryn O'Sullivan (ed.) *Minority Religions under Irish Law: Islam in National and International Context* 34, 37 (Brill, 2019) notes the text of the Constitution emerged as a 'political compromise between rival strands of nationalist and republican thought'. *See also* Eoin Daly, *Religion, Law and the Irish State* (Clarus, 2012) and Gerard Hogan, 'De Valera, the Constitution and the Historians' 40 *Irish Jurist* 291 (2005).
61. For a discussion of the historical development of Art. 44, *see* Dermot Keogh, 'The Irish Constitutional Revolution: An Analysis of the Making of the Constitution' 35 *Administration* 4, 4–84 (1985).
62. Siobhan Mullally & Darren O'Donovan, 'Religion and Ireland's "Public Squares": Education, the Family and Expanding Equality Claims' (April) *Public Law* 284, 287 (2011) observe: 'The requirements of public order and morality have been interpreted strictly, as the role of constitutional protection has been viewed as one of facilitating religious practice and religious ways of life.'
63. *See* Oran Doyle, 'Article 44: Privileging the Rights of the Religious' in Eoin Carolan & Oran Doyle (eds) *The Irish Constitution: Governance and Values* 476 (Roundhall, 2008) for a consideration of the protection afforded to non-religious world views.

such State-funded schools.[64] A prohibition on the endowment of religions is also carried out in Article 44.2.2°.[65]

29. In *Quinn's Supermarket v. Attorney General,*[66] the 'leading case on the constitutional protection of the right to free profession and practice of religion',[67] the Irish Supreme Court (IESC) considered a constitutional challenge to ministerial regulations which sought to regulate the opening hours of butcher shops and, in doing so, sought to make an exception for Jewish butcher shops with regard to the Sabbath. It was argued that such differential treatment in favour of a religious minority constituted discrimination on the grounds of religious 'belief, profession or status' pursuant to Article 44.2.3°.

30. Delivering its judgment, the Supreme Court concluded that the principal purpose of Article 44.2 was to guarantee 'freedom of conscience' and ruled that Article 44.2.3° prohibited not only negative discrimination but, at least prima facie, all forms of differential treatment based on religion, including 'positive' discrimination.[68] As a result, Daly explains, 'discrimination was not solely defined as "discrimination against"'.[69] Despite this, however, the Court held that in certain circumstances, religious discrimination may be valid to 'secure or encourage the free profession and practice of religion'.[70] In determining the validity or otherwise of the discrimination, the Court added that it would be important to consider the nature of the practice effected as well as the level of interference involved. Justice Walsh held:

> Any law which by virtue of the generality of its application would by its effect restrict or prevent the free profession and practice of religion … would be invalid having regard to the provisions of the Constitution, unless it … saved

---

64. Article 44.2.4° states: 'Legislation providing State aid for schools shall not discriminate between schools under the management of different religious denominations, nor be such as to affect prejudicially the right of any child to attend a school receiving public money without attending religious instruction at that school.' *See* Part IX for more.
65. *See* Part VIII for more. Citing the case of *Campaign to Separate Church and State v. Minister for Education* (1998) 2 ILRM 81, Siobhan Mullally & Darren O'Donovan, 'Religion and Ireland's "Public Squares": Education, the Family and Expanding Equality Claims' (April) *Public Law* 284, 286 (2011) note 'Where conflict has arisen, Irish constitutional jurisprudence has consistently given priority to freedom of religion over other constitutional principles such as non-discrimination and non-endowment.'
66. [1972] IR 1.
67. Siobhan Mullally & Darren O'Donovan, 'Religion and Ireland's "Public Squares": Education, the Family and Expanding Equality Claims' (April) *Public Law* 284, 286 (2011).
68. The court also noted at 23: '[Article 44.1] acknowledges that the homage of public worship is due to Almighty God but it does so in terms which do not confine the benefit of that acknowledgment to members of the Christian faith.'
69. Eoin Daly, 'Accommodating Religious Minorities in Ireland: The Constitutional Framework' in Kathryn O'Sullivan (ed.) *Minority Religions under Irish Law: Islam in National and International Context* 34, 45 (Brill, 2019).
70. [1972] IR 1, 34.

> from such restriction or prevention the practice of religion of the person or persons who would otherwise be so restricted or prevented.[71]

31. The court concluded that the exemption for Kosher butcher shops from closing hours went beyond what was 'necessary' for the free practice of religion and was thus unconstitutional.[72]

32. On one interpretation, the case would suggest 'that all religious exemptions in statute are unconstitutional unless constitutionally required by religious freedom'.[73] Despite this, it has been observed that it is 'unlikely' that in practice the decision would prevent the Oireachtas from enacting religious accommodations.[74] Indeed, to the contrary, as Whyte posits, the case could be viewed as an authority for the fact that 'the State is obliged … to grant an exemption to religious interests from laws of general applicability in the interests of ensuring the free practice of religion'.[75]

33. Yet, despite the passage of almost fifty years since the decision in Quinn's Supermarket was handed down – and notwithstanding the fact that 'religious discourse has long had a role in the public sphere in Ireland'[76] – the scope of the decision, at a practical level, continues to be somewhat unclear. It remains to be seen, for example, whether it could be relied upon to successfully protect the claims of members of religious organisations who wish to seek recognition or protection for obscure (or potentially otherwise illegal) religious rituals. It has been recently pointed out that:

> while the *Quinn's Supermarket* judgment might suggest a potentially fruitful constitutional framework for the protection of religious freedom, there has been practically no litigation surrounding religious practices of the kind that have been the subject of legal dispute and political controversy in neighbouring states.[77]

---

71. [1972] IR 1, 23.
72. *See* Oran Doyle, 'Article 44: Privileging the Rights of the Religious' in Eoin Carolan & Oran Doyle (eds) *The Irish Constitution: Governance and Values* 476, 479–481 (Roundhall, 2008).
73. Which, Eoin Daly, 'Accommodating Religious Minorities in Ireland: The Constitutional Framework' in Kathryn O'Sullivan (ed.) *Minority Religions under Irish Law: Islam in National and International Context* 34, 46 (Brill, 2019) notes, 'thereby removes religious accommodation from political choice'.
74. Eoin Daly, 'Accommodating Religious Minorities in Ireland: The Constitutional Framework' in Kathryn O'Sullivan (ed.) *Minority Religions under Irish Law: Islam in National and International Context* 34, 46 (Brill, 2019). He notes that '[r]eligious freedom is likely to be given a very broad definition, which encompasses the broad interests of religious groups in being facilitated in religious practice, in particular by being exempted from regulatory burdens'. In *Quinn's Supermarket*, as noted above, the extensive nature of the exemption was considered excessive.
75. Gerard Whyte, 'On the Meaning of "Religion" under the Irish Constitution' in Eoin Carolan & Oran Doyle (eds) *The Irish Constitution: Governance and Values* 446, 447 (Roundhall, 2008).
76. Siobhan Mullally & Darren O'Donovan, 'Religion and Ireland's "Public Squares": Education, the Family and Expanding Equality Claims' (April) *Public Law* 284, 284 (2011).
77. Eoin Daly, 'Accommodating Religious Minorities in Ireland: The Constitutional Framework' in K O'Sullivan (ed.) *Minority Religions under Irish Law: Islam in National and International Context*

34. That said, in *McGrath and Ó Ruairc v. Trustees of Maynooth College*, the constitutional prohibition on religious discrimination was also considered by the Supreme Court.[78] The plaintiffs claimed they were the victims of discrimination, having been dismissed from their posts as college lecturers in a Catholic college due to their laicisation and disagreement with Catholic teaching. The Supreme Court found against the plaintiffs and reiterated the ability of a religion to protect its ethos from attack. Justice Henchy held:

> The constitutional provision invoked here [Article 44.2.3] must be construed in the terms of its purpose. In proscribing disabilities and discriminations at the hands of the State on the ground of religious profession, belief or status, *the primary aim of the constitutional guarantee is to give vitality, independence and freedom to religion*. To construe the provision literally, without due regard to its underlying objective, would lead to a sapping and debilitation of the freedom and independence given by the Constitution to the doctrinal and organisational requirements and proscriptions which are inherent in all organised religions. Far from eschewing the internal disabilities and discriminations which flow from the tenets of a particular religion, the State must on occasion recognise and buttress them. For such disabilities and discrimination do not derive from the State; it cannot be said that it is the State that imposed or made them; they are part of the texture and essence of the particular religion; so the State, in order to comply with the spirit and purpose inherent in this constitutional guarantee, may justifiably lend its weight to what may be thought to be disabilities and discriminations deriving from within a particular religion.[79]

35. In re Article 26 and the Employment Equality Bill 1996, the Supreme Court again restated its position:

> It is constitutionally permissible to make distinctions or discriminations on grounds of religious profession, belief or status insofar – but only in so far – as this may be necessary to give life and reality to the guarantee of the free profession and practice of religion in the Constitution.[80]

36. Furthermore, it is clear from the Supreme Court decision in *McGee v. Attorney General* that nobody ought to be coerced or compelled to act contrary to their conscience, 'in so far as the practice of religion is concerned'.[81] The Court emphasised that Article 44 protected freedom of conscience only 'so far as the exercise, practice or profession of religion is concerned'.[82]

34, 50 (Brill, 2019). Siobhan Mullally & Darren O'Donovan, 'Religion and Ireland's "Public Squares": Education, the Family and Expanding Equality Claims' (April) *Public Law* 284, 287 (2011) also note: 'The accommodation of religious claims has given rise to only limited case law to date in Ireland.'

78. [1979] ILRM 166.
79. [1979] ILRM 166, 187 (emphasis added).
80. [1997] 2 IR 321.
81. [1974] 1 IR 281 at [316]–[317].
82. [1974] 1 IR 281 at [317]. Thus matters of social conscience were not protected.

37. In *Murphy v. Independent Radio and Television Commission*, meanwhile, the Supreme Court was willing to uphold a prohibition on religious advertising.[83] Notwithstanding that the ban amounted to an apparent restriction on religious expression, it was regarded as necessary in order to avoid potential unrest and divisiveness.[84]

38. Perhaps unsurprisingly, given the broader socio-political and historical context within which Article 44 was constructed and interpreted by the Irish courts, it has been observed that 'Irish constitutional doctrine, reflecting the text itself, has oscillated between principles of neutrality and recognition as regards religion.'[85] Similarly, as Mullally and O'Donovan note:

> accommodation and recognition of religious claims has sometimes been viewed as an intrinsic component of Ireland's cultural heritage, a reflection of the State's national identity. At other times, however, restrictions on religious expression have been viewed as necessary to safeguard the impartiality of the State.[86]

39. Despite Ireland's ever-increasing multiculturalism, the lack of litigation involving religion, even in recent decades, has meant few opportunities for the Irish Superior Courts to develop a coherent position on various issues which are likely arising at the grassroots level.

---

83. [1999] 1 IR 12.
84. For more on religious advertising, *see* Part XI Ch. 2.
85. Eoin Daly, 'Accommodating Religious Minorities in Ireland: The Constitutional Framework' in Kathryn O'Sullivan (ed.) *Minority Religions under Irish Law: Islam in National and International Context* 34, 53 (Brill, 2019). He describes the 'recognition approach' as one which 'recognises religion as a public good, and supports active state intervention aimed at recognising and sustaining religion – albeit in a pluralistic sense – as a part of the social fabric'. By contrast, the 'neutrality approach' is one in which 'religion is understood as a protected sphere of private activity, in which the State may not generally intrude, whether for benign reasons or otherwise'.
86. Siobhan Mullally & Darren O'Donovan, 'Religion and Ireland's "Public Squares": Education, the Family and Expanding Equality Claims' (April) *Public Law* 284, 291 (2011). *See also* Oran Doyle, 'Article 44: Privileging the Rights of the Religious' in Eoin Carolan & Oran Doyle (eds) *The Irish Constitution: Governance and Values* 476 (Roundhall, 2008).

Chapter 2. Collective Religious Freedom

40. As noted above, collective religious freedom is also recognised under Irish law, with religious groups sometimes benefitting from denominationally specific provisions[87] or, more commonly, from general rules, including those pertaining to equality legislation. These protections will be considered in the relevant part of the monograph.

87. *See* examples above.

Chapter 3. Organisational Religious Freedom

41. For the purposes of this chapter, the focus will be placed on the freedoms enjoyed by religious organisations themselves.[88] Pursuant to Article 44.2.5°, denominational autonomy is guaranteed for religious organisations. It provides: 'Every religious denomination shall have the right to manage its own affairs, own, acquire and administer property, movable and immovable, and maintain institutions for religious or charitable purposes.' Reflecting on this provision, Daly observes:

> Barring issues of public order, the internal structure and form of denominations appear to be constitutionally protected against any imposition of statist and secular policy agendas. This would also clearly apply to any attempt to administer or regulate religious rituals, practices or functions or to bring the 'management' of denominational 'affairs', in any other way, within the remit of public authority.[89]

42. Article 44.2.6°, moreover, provides constitutional protection to the property of religious denominations, with such protections viewed as stronger than those afforded to private property generally under Articles 40.3 and 43. It states: 'The property of any religious denomination or any educational institution shall not be diverted save for necessary works of public utility and on payment of compensation.'[90]

43. To date, the denominational autonomy principle has attracted little academic or judicial comment and has yet to form the basis of a successful constitutional challenge to legislation or state actions.[91] However, notwithstanding this lack of engagement, it is interesting to consider which purported religious organisations might, in an appropriate case, benefit from the protections provided in Article 44.2.5° and

88. In the context of the Irish Constitution, discussed below, Eoin Daly, *Religion, Law and the Irish State* 388 (Clarus, 2012) notes 'the significance of a separate constitutional denominational autonomy, distinct from individual religious freedom, is unclear'.
89. Eoin Daly, *Religion, Law and the Irish State* 384–385 (Clarus, 2012). However, *see* 382–384, 410–421 for consideration of s. 99(3) of the Charities Act 2009 regarding the regulation of mass cards. Note, also, religious organisations may be subject to indirect regulation for the purposes, for example, of charity law. *See* Part III Ch. 1 for more.
90. As Gerard Whyte, 'On the Meaning of "Religion" under the Irish Constitution' in Eoin Carolan & Oran Doyle (eds) *The Irish Constitution: Governance and Values* 446, 447 (Roundhall, 2008) explains, this provides superior protection since the 'property rights of others may be regulated by more general principles of social justice and may have to be reconciled with the more indeterminate "exigences of the common good". Nor is it necessarily the case that compensation always has to be paid where the property rights of non-religious bodies are curtailed'.
91. Nevertheless, in *McGrath and Ó Ruairc v. Trustees of Maynooth College* [1979] ILRM 166, Siobhan Mullally & Darren O'Donovan, 'Religion and Ireland's "Public Squares": Education, the Family and Expanding Equality Claims' (April) *Public Law* 284, 287 (2011) note: '[t]he court ... was markedly deferential to the right of religious denominations to manage their own affairs, including in matters of employment'.

Article 44.2.6° bearing in mind that the Irish Constitution provides no explicit definition of 'religion'.[92] Pursuant to Article 44, as originally enacted in 1937, the 'special position' of the Roman Catholic Church was recognised under Article 44. In a now-deleted reference, it acknowledged the 'special position of the Holy Catholic Apostolic and Roman Church as the guardian of the Faith professed by the great majority of the citizens' and 'recognised' other minority denominations including the Church of Ireland, the Presbyterian Church in Ireland, the Methodist Church in Ireland, the Religious Society of Friends in Ireland, the Jewish Congregations and 'the other religious denominations existing' in Ireland. While the reference to the 'special position' of the Catholic Church was not considered to have legal effect,[93] it was nevertheless removed with the Fifth Amendment to the Constitution in Ireland in 1972.[94] Although Whyte notes that the religions listed must 'conclusively be deemed to be religious for the purposes of the Constitution',[95] questions remain as to what criteria will be applied to determine the status of other prospective religious bodies.

44. Recent research has highlighted the proliferation of small religious bodies securing recognition under the Civil Registration Act 2004 (as amended) for the purpose of marriage solemnisation.[96] Section 45 of the 2004 Act (as amended) defines a 'religious body' as 'an organised group of people members of which meet regularly for common religious worship'. While Whyte notes 'the reference to "worship" in the definition arguably implies belief in a Supreme Being',[97] little else appears clear as to what precise criteria are being used to determine whether an

92. Gerard Whyte, 'On the Meaning of "Religion" under the Irish Constitution' in Eoin Carolan & Oran Doyle (eds) *The Irish Constitution: Governance and Values* 446 (Roundhall, 2008).
93. This was acknowledged, albeit *obiter*, by Geoghegan J in *Ó Beoláin v. Fahy* [2001] 2 IR 279. *See also* Daithí Ó Corráin, 'Articles 41 and 44: Minority Religious Opinion 1937–1986' in Eoin Carolan & Oran Doyle (eds) *The Irish Constitution: Governance and Values* 53 (Roundhall, 2008).
94. Siobhan Mullally & Darren O'Donovan, 'Religion and Ireland's "Public Squares": Education, the Family and Expanding Equality Claims' (April) *Public Law* 284, 287 (2011) note: 'The amendment was largely a response to the outbreak of conflict in Northern Ireland and reflected a desire to signal a greater openness to religious minorities.' *See also* Niamh Ní Leathlobhair & Donal K. Coffey, 'Article 44.1 and the "Special Position" of the Catholic Church in the Irish Constitution, 1937–1972' in Kevin Costello & Niamh Howlin (eds) *Law and Religion in Ireland, 1700–1970* 357-384 (Palgrave MacMillan, 2021).
95. Gerard Whyte, 'On the Meaning of "Religion" under the Irish Constitution' in Eoin Carolan & Oran Doyle (eds) *The Irish Constitution: Governance and Values* 446, 450 (Roundhall, 2008).
96. A large number of smaller religions appear to have secured recognition under the 2004 Act (as amended) with over 100 religious bodies recorded on the register of bodies authorised to solemnise marriages previously published by the General Register Office, albeit that there appears no statutory basis for the existence of such a register, *see* http://www.welfare.ie/en/pressoffice/pdf/bodiesauthorisedtosolemisemarriage.pdf (accessed 3 Apr. 2017). Note also, it is unknown when this list was last officially updated. A significant number of religions represented on the register of solemnisers only have one solemniser registered, *see*, https://www.welfare.ie/en/downloads/RegisterOfSolemnisers.pdf (accessed 6 Jun. 2023). For discussion of the implications of this trend in the context of training of solemnisers, in particular, *see* Susan Leahy & Kathryn O'Sullivan, 'Changing Conceptions of Marriage in Ireland: Law and Practice' 30(3) *Child and Family Law Quarterly* 279 (2018).
97. Gerard Whyte, 'On the Meaning of "Religion" under the Irish Constitution' in Eoin Carolan & Oran Doyle (eds) *The Irish Constitution: Governance and Values* 446, 449 note 10 (Roundhall, 2008).

organisation is 'religious' or not.[98] It seems the application process for recognition as a religion for the purposes of nominating a solemniser under the 2004 Act merely requires the body concerned to provide details of its constitution (including a description of the organisation structure), a brief description of its belief system, confirmation of registration as a charity (if applicable), a copy of the credentials of the nominee and a certificate to the effect that the form of marriage ceremony complies with the legal requirements for a valid marriage.[99] Given that, (as Whyte argues) legislative recognition – such as that afforded to the Baptist Union of Ireland and the Plymouth Brethren under the now repealed Adoption Act 1952 – would 'clearly bolster the claims' of a denomination to be recognised as a religion for the purposes of the Constitution and Irish law generally,[100] recognition pursuant to the 2004 Act (as amended) would likely prove similarly helpful.[101] Nevertheless, it remains to be seen how the law develops in this area and precisely what is required of prospective religious denominations in order to avail of the protections afforded under Article 44 in particular.

98. Given the absence of a comprehensive legislative definition, Gerard Whyte, 'On the Meaning of "Religion" under the Irish Constitution' in Eoin Carolan & Oran Doyle (eds) *The Irish Constitution: Governance and Values* 446, notes at 450–451 (Roundhall, 2008) 'If the Constitution is only of limited guidance in relation to the definition of religion, legislation is even less helpful … .'
99. *See* Susan Leahy & Kathryn O'Sullivan, 'Changing Conceptions of Marriage in Ireland: Law and Practice' 30(3) *Child and Family Law Quarterly* 279 (2018).
100. Gerard Whyte, 'On the Meaning of "Religion" under the Irish Constitution' in Eoin Carolan & Oran Doyle (eds) *The Irish Constitution: Governance and Values* 446, 452 (Roundhall, 2008).
101. *See also* Part III Ch. 1 below for consideration of how religion is defined under Irish charities law.

Part III. Legal Status of Religious Communities

Chapter 1. Formal Status of Religious Communities

§1. Absence of Established Church

45. The Disestablishment Act of 1869 disestablished the Church of Ireland in Ireland.[102] Since then, religions have been legally 'private' in the jurisdiction. Notwithstanding that significant pressure was brought to bear on the drafters of the 1937 Constitution to formally establish the Roman Catholic Church, such status was not afforded to any religion.[103] As a result, there continues to be no formally established church in Ireland. Furthermore, and perhaps surprisingly given its strong Roman Catholic tradition, Ireland has never enjoyed or possessed a Concordat with the Catholic Church or the Vatican.

46. Unlike other so-called separationist or secular systems, however, the Irish Constitution of 1937 is interesting in so far as it does not specifically or expressly forbid the 'establishment' of religions. While a ban on the establishment of religions was initially included in the Government of Ireland Act 1920, such a prohibition was not included in the Anglo-Irish Treaty of 1921, nor was it subsequently included in the Constitution of the Irish Free State in 1922 or in Bunreacht na hÉireann in 1937. It remains open to speculation as to why the prohibition was dropped. In Campaign to *Separate Church and State v. Minister for Education*, Barrington J suggested:

> presumably it was because the combined effect of the ban on the endowment of any religion and the prohibition of the granting of any preference on the grounds

102. *See* Keith Robbins, 'The Disestablishment of the Church of Ireland' in Kevin Costello & Niamh Howlin (eds) *Law and Religion in Ireland, 1700–1970* 239–256 (Palgrave MacMillan, 2021).

103. Barry Sullivan, 'The Irish Constitution: Some Reflections from Abroad' in Eoin Carolan & Oran Doyle (eds) *The Irish Constitution: Governance and Values* 1, 10 (Roundhall, 2008) notes: 'Given the influence of the Catholic Church and its place in Irish society in 1937, and, indeed, for many years thereafter, one wonders whether there would have been much to gain … by going beyond what was in the Constitution to create a formal "establishment".' *See also* Dermot Keogh & Andrew McCarthy, *The Making of the 1937 Constitution* (Mercer, 2007) and Eoin Daly, *Religion, Law and the Irish State* 28–33 (Clarus, 2012).

of religious belief or status was to make an express ban on establishment unnecessary.[104]

47. Given the lack of a formally established church, all churches in Ireland are considered voluntary and unincorporated associations.[105] Notwithstanding the flexibility this presents for religious organisations or entities in terms of how they wish to structure themselves, it has been observed that it has led to 'complexity and lack of homogeneity in addressing the question of religious entities in Ireland as legal persons'.[106] Moreover, Colton notes: 'Since so many church-related cases have been settled out of court many of the unclear issues in this area have not been settled.'[107]

48. There is no legal requirement that religious groups or organisations register with the government, nor is there any formal mechanism in place for government recognition of a religious organisation or group. In keeping with Article 44.2.5°, under which denominational autonomy is guaranteed for religious organisations,[108] the relationship between the Irish State and religious bodies has been described as of a 'markedly … laissez-faire ethos'.[109] Nevertheless, there are legal mechanisms in place in Ireland requiring religious groups to register for specific purposes, including for the solemnisation of marriage or to secure charitable status.

§2. Civil Registration Act 2004 (As Amended)

49. Pursuant to the Civil Registration Act 2004 (as amended), three different types of marriage ceremony may be recognised: a civil ceremony conducted by a civil registrar who is employed by the Health Service Executive; a religious ceremony solemnised by a registered solemniser from a religious body; or a secular ceremony solemnised by a registered solemniser from a secular body.[110]

50. In order to be a registered solemniser for religious wedding ceremonies, one must be a nominated member of a religious body who is included on the register of solemnisers.[111] Would-be or prospective solemnisers cannot self-nominate, and all nominations must be approved by the Registrar General. It remains unclear precisely what this approval process entails, whether approval is freely given or

104. [1998] 3 IR 321. The prohibition on endowment of religions will be considered further in Part VIII.
105. The right to form such 'associations' is protected by Art. 40.6.1° of the Irish Constitution. *See* Ch. 4 for more.
106. Paul Colton, 'Religious Entities as Legal Persons in Ireland' in Lars Friedner (ed.) *Churches and Other Religious Organisations as Legal Persons: Proceedings of the 17th Meeting of the European Consortium for Church and State Research* 138 (Peeters, 17–20 Nov. 2005).
107. Paul Colton, 'Religious Entities as Legal Persons in Ireland' in Lars Friedner (ed.) *Churches and Other Religious Organisations as Legal Persons: Proceedings of the 17th Meeting of the European Consortium for Church and State Research* 138 (Peeters, 17–20 Nov. 2005).
108. *See* Part II Ch. 3 and Part III Ch. 2.
109. Eoin Daly, *Religion, Law and the Irish State* 386 (Clarus, 2012).
110. *See* Part X Ch. 1 for more on marriage formalities.
111. Section 51(3)(c).

whether criteria are applied to determine the suitability and qualifications of the proposed solemniser. Moreover, while a person must be nominated by a religious body, a very loose definition of what this might be is provided. Section 45 of the Civil Registration Act 2004 (as amended) merely states a 'religious body' is 'an organised group of people members of which meet regularly for common religious worship'.[112]

51. This sweeping definition stands in marked contrast to the much more detailed criteria laid down by section 45A of the 2004 Act (as amended)[113] in order to secure recognition of an organisation as a secular body. It provides that a body will be a secular body if it has at least fifty members, has been in existence for a continuous period of at least five years and has principal objects that are secular, ethical and humanist. The definition adds that the members of the body must meet regularly in relation to their beliefs and in furtherance of these objects and must not have any rules regarding marriage or the solemnisation of marriages that are in contravention of the requirements of the 2004 Act or any other enactment or the rule of law. It must also be demonstrated to the satisfaction of the Registrar General that the body has appropriate procedures in writing for selecting, training and accrediting members as fit and proper persons to solemnise marriages.[114]

52. Interestingly, unlike in England and Wales, there is no concept of a registered venue for religious marriage ceremonies in Ireland. The baseline requirement is that in order to be regarded as suitable for a marriage ceremony, a venue must be a 'place that is open to the public'.[115] Once this criterion is met, religious and secular solemnisers are free to choose the venues in which marriage ceremonies will be conducted.[116]

§3. Charities Act 2009 (As Amended)

53. Despite not being required to do so, religious bodies may wish to seek formal recognition as a charitable organisation in Ireland. According to the Charities Regulator, there are more than 11,500 charities on the Register of Charities.[117] Although long governed by the common law, the law of charities in Ireland saw a welcome codification with the introduction of the Charities Act 2009 (as amended). Pursuant to section 2 of the 2009 Act (as amended), 'charitable organisation' is

---

112. *See* Part II Ch. 3.
113. As inserted by s. 3 of the Civil Registration (Amendment) Act 2012.
114. Furthermore, the body must maintain a register of its members, have secured charitable status for tax purposes and not have the making of profit as one of its principal objects. *See* s. 45A(2) (as inserted by s. 3 of the Civil Registration (Amendment) Act 2012) for a list of what does *not* constitute a secular body. *See* Part X Ch. 1 for more.
115. Section 51(2A). For more, *see* Kathryn O'Sullivan, 'Location, Location, Location: The Future of Weddings Law in Ireland and England' 43(3) *Journal of Social Welfare and Family Law* (2021) (forthcoming).
116. *See* Part X Ch. 1 for more.
117. *See*, https://www.charitiesregulator.ie/en/information-for-the-public/search-the-register-of-charities (accessed 8 Jun. 2023).

defined to include a body corporate or an unincorporated body of persons that promotes a charitable purpose provided that, under its constitution, it is required to apply all of its property (both real and personal) in furtherance of that purpose.[118] Gifts for the advancement of religion, long recognised in Ireland under the common law,[119] continue to be regarded as gifts for a charitable purpose as confirmed by section 3(1), thereby benefitting from tax relief.[120] Again reflecting the common law position, section 3(2) states a purpose shall not be a charitable purpose unless it is of 'public benefit'.[121]

54. The public benefit requirement has traditionally been applied somewhat leniently in the context of gifts for the advancement of religion.[122] This approach is, for the most part, replicated in the 2009 Act (as amended). Section 3(4) states: 'It shall be presumed, unless the contrary is proved, that a gift for the advancement of religion is of public benefit.'[123] Although now repealed, section 45(1) of the Charities Act 1961 originally provided that once it was established that a trust advances a religion, it could be conclusively presumed that there was a public benefit; this presumption has been slightly diluted. Instead of providing a conclusive presumption, the 2009 Act (as amended) carries a rebuttable presumption that gifts for the advancement of religion are of public benefit. Section 3(5) of the 2009 Act (as amended) provides that the Charities Regulatory Authority may now make a determination that a gift for the advancement of religion is not of public benefit. However, it may not do so without the consent of the Attorney General. Where such a conclusion is reached by the Charities Regulator or the Attorney General, it cannot be appealed to the Charity Appeals Tribunal.

55. In order to benefit from charitable status, a detailed application must be submitted to the Charities Regulatory Authority.[124] Although the Charities Act 2009 (as amended) does not carry a definition of religion, existing case law appears to speak to a need for the religion to demonstrate belief in a 'Supreme Being' and faith and worship of that 'Supreme Being' with such requirements recently reiterated by the Charities Regulator.[125] The Charities Regulator adds: 'To advance religion, your

118. An exception is included in the context of religious organisations or communities who may also expend money on accommodation and care of members of the organisation or community.
119. *See*, for example, *Maguire v. AG* [1943] IR 238; *Bank of Ireland Trustee Co. Ltd v. Attorney General* [1957] IR 257.
120. Subsection (6) provides 'A charitable gift for the purpose of the advancement of religion shall have effect, and the terms upon which it is given shall be construed, in accordance with the laws, canons, ordinances and tenets of the religion concerned.'
121. As established in *Oppenheim v. Tobacco Securities* [1951] AC 297.
122. *See O'Hanlon v. Logue* [1906] 1 IR 247 where the court held that a gift for the saying of masses whether in public or private was a valid charitable gift. *See also Bank of Ireland Trustee Co. Ltd v. Attorney General* [1957] IR 257 where a gift for the repair and improvement of the convent of a contemplative order of nuns was upheld.
123. In this regard, the Irish protection goes further than that in many other jurisdictions.
124. Section 39(3). *See*, https://www.charitiesregulator.ie/en/information-for-charities/apply-for-charitable-status (accessed 8 Jun. 2023). *See also* Part V Ch. 1 for more on the Charities Regulator.
125. This is confirmed in Charities Regulator, *What Is a Charity*, 7 available at https://www.charitiesregulator.ie/media/1544/what-is-a-charity-rev-001.pdf (accessed 8 Jun. 2023). *See also In Re South*

organisation's work must support a religion that contains the two core elements outlined, but it does not necessarily need to be a religious body.'[126]

56. Once it is established to the satisfaction of the Charities Regulator that the organisation or body meets the (albeit vague) requirements to be recognised as a religion, it then moves to consider its application for charitable status. Section 39(5) sets out a comprehensive list of requirements for an application. A religious body, for example, must describe the particulars of how the organisation advances its religion and what the plans of the organisation or trustees are for funding activities in furtherance of its objects or the objects of the trust. Where the Authority makes a decision to refuse an application under this section, section 39(10) provides that it shall, as soon as may be thereafter, notify the applicant in writing of the decision and the reasons for the decision as well as the applicant's entitlement under section 45(1) to appeal the decision. It is an offence for unregistered charitable organisations to carry out activities in the State.[127]

57. While traditionally, charitable status and tax exemptions were dealt with together, these issues have since been decoupled under Irish law. Therefore, if a religious community wishes to seek a tax exemption, they are required to also register with the Revenue Commissioners of Ireland and obtain official Charitable Tax Exemption status.[128]

58. Finally, it is worthwhile to note that section 3(10) of the 2009 Act (as amended) states a gift is not a gift for the advancement of religion if it is made to or for the benefit of an organisation or cult, the principal object of which is the making of profit, or that employs oppressive psychological manipulation of its followers, or for the purpose of gaining new followers.

Place Ethical Society [1980] 3 ALL ER 918. *See also* Oonagh Breen & Philip Smith, *Law of Charities in Ireland* (Bloomsbury, 2019). Note, the Law Reform Committee of the Law Society has recommended that clarification be provided on whether the legal definition of religion extends beyond supreme beings to embrace a belief in principles or ethics. They were divided on which approach should be favoured, however. No clarity is provided on this issue by the Act.

126. Charities Regulator, *What Is a Charity*, 7 available at, https://www.charitiesregulator.ie/media/1544/what-is-a-charity-rev-001.pdf (accessed 8 Jun. 2023). *See also* Charities Regulator, *Charity Classification Guide,* 17 available at, https://www.charitiesregulator.ie/media/4563/charities-regulator-classification-guide.pdf (accessed 8 Jun. 2023).

127. Section 41 of the 2009 Act.

128. *See*, https://www.revenue.ie/en/companies-and-charities/charities-and-sports-bodies/charitable-tax-exemption/index.aspx (accessed 8 Jun. 2023).

Chapter 2. Autonomy of Religious Communities

59. In general, religions in Ireland are viewed as private voluntary associations whose relationship with their members is based on a contract.[129] In this context, it is unsurprising that, as discussed in Part II Chapter 3, considerable denominational autonomy is guaranteed for religions in the State under the Irish Constitution. In addition to Article 44.1, wherein the State pledges to 'honour and respect religion', Article 44.2.5° further states: 'Every religious denomination shall have the right to manage its own affairs, own, acquire and administer property, movable and immovable, and maintain institutions for religious or charitable purposes.' Thus, as Henchy J observed in *McGrath and Ó Ruairc v. Trustees of Maynooth College*, one of the 'primary aim[s]' of Article 44 was 'to give independence, vitality and freedom to religion'.[130]

60. Notwithstanding that religious communities are not required to register as religions in Ireland, religious communities may choose, for example, to register as charities pursuant to the Charities Act 2009, as noted above. All charities registered in this manner are then listed on the publicly accessible Register of Charities.[131] To the extent that a religious organisation may have secured charitable status, it will then be subject to potentially much more rigorous oversight.[132] Whether religious or otherwise, all organisations on the Register of Charities must provide annual information on their activities to the Charities Regulatory Authority. The 2009 Act requires charitable organisations to keep proper books of accounts and to comply with certain annual reporting and auditing requirements.[133] The level of reporting and auditing required depends on the level of resources of the organisation.

---

129. *The State (Colquhoun) v. D'Arcy* [1936] IR 641.
130. *McGrath and Ó Ruairc v. Trustees of Maynooth College* [1979] ILRM 166, at 187. Note, in *Quinn's Supermarket v. Attorney General* [1972] IR 1 at 11 the Supreme Court held that the 'overall purpose' of Art. 44 is 'freedom of practice of religion'.
131. *See*, https://www.charitiesregulator.ie/en/information-for-the-public/search-the-register-of-charities (accessed 29 Feb. 2024).
132. However, as Eoin Daly, 'Accommodating Religious Minorities in Ireland: The Constitutional Framework' in Kathryn O'Sullivan (ed.) *Minority Religions under Irish Law: Islam in National and International Context* 34, 36 (Brill, 2019) notes 'there has been little political appetite to legally regulate religions or bring their administration within public remit'.
133. *See* Part 3 of the 2009 Act.

Chapter 3. Fundamental Rights and Religious Communities

61. Issues regarding fundamental rights and religious communities were addressed in Part II and are also noted in Part IV Chapter 1 below.

Chapter 4. Contractual Religious Freedom

62. As noted, churches in Ireland are considered voluntary associations. Given this status, Sullivan P in the High Court case of *State (Colquhoun) v. D'Arcy*, explained the status of a church not established by law as:

> the status of a voluntary association the members of which subscribe or assent to certain rules and regulations and bind themselves to each other to conform to certain laws and principles, the obligation to such conformity and observance resting wholly in the mutual contract of the members enforceable only as a matter of contract by the ordinary tribunal of the land.[134]

63. In general, therefore, religious bodies and their internal laws are regulated by private rather than public law. Given the constitutional separation of church and state, moreover, the rules of churches in the jurisdiction are not given statutory recognition.[135] Colton explains, for example, '[i]n civil law terms, the Church of Ireland is a consensual society, and internal Church law is contractual in nature, binding its adherents voluntarily'.[136]

134. [1936] IR 641 citing Barry J in *O'Keeffe v. Cullen* (citation omitted). For more, *see* Paul Colton, 'Religious Entities as Legal Persons in Ireland' in Lars Friedner (ed.) *Churches and Other Religious Organisations as Legal Persons: Proceedings of the 17th Meeting of the European Consortium for Church and State Research* 125–139 (Peeters, 17–20 Nov. 200).
135. In the past, in particular, legislation was introduced to bring civil law in line with Church rules, for example, in the case of nullity with the Matrimonial Causes and Marriage Law (Ireland) (Amendment) Act 1870.
136. Paul Colton, *Sources of Law of the Church of Ireland: Identification, Investigation and Reform* 48 (PhD Thesis, Cardiff University, 2013).

Part IV. International, Transnational, Regional Effects on Religious Communities

Introduction

64. This part will seek to highlight the main international, transnational and regional laws affecting religious communities in Ireland. In particular, it will place a focus on the United Nations (UN) Declaration on Human Rights and the European Convention for the Protection of Human Rights and Fundamental Freedoms. In considering this part, it is also important to have regard to the role of the Irish Human Rights and Equality Commission (IHREC), which is discussed further in Part V Chapter 1.

Chapter 1. International Law Affecting Religious Communities

§1. Introduction to International Law

65. First coined by English philosopher Jeremy Bentham (1748–1832), international law refers to a body of globally agreed legal rules, norms, and (often minimum) standards that apply between sovereign states and other internationally legally recognised entities. It may serve to influence domestic decision-making and legislation as well as frequently playing an important role in framing debates regarding controversial issues of a national and international nature.

66. In recognising international law, states may choose between two approaches. They may choose to recognise the terms of international treaties and conventions as a part of domestic law in a 'monist approach'. Alternatively, as is the situation in Ireland, they may take a 'dualist approach'. Under this latter approach, states may recognise the specific terms of international treaties and conventions as obligations under international law while simultaneously withholding recognition of resulting rights under domestic law unless and until such obligations are embodied in domestic legislation. Thus, international agreements which are ratified by Ireland are not, of themselves, self-executing. The provisions of the international covenants on human rights cannot, therefore, be invoked before or directly enforced by the courts, and they do not take effect as domestic law until such time as they are legislatively enacted.

67. This dualist approach may be traced to Article 29.6 of the Irish Constitution, which provides that 'no international agreement shall be part of the domestic law of the State save as may be determined by the Oireachtas'. This has been interpreted as effectively preventing the Irish courts from giving effect to any international agreement which could be regarded as contrary to Irish law or which would grant rights or impose obligations additional to those of domestic law. It appears unlikely that any initiatives will be taken to alter this approach.[137]

§2. United Nations: An Overview

68. The UN is an intergovernmental body established to promote international cooperation. Comprising of 193 Member States, it may be divided into six principal organs, including the General Assembly, the Security Council, the Economic and Social Council, the International Court of Justice and the Secretariat.[138] One of the key purposes of the UN, as confirmed by the UN Charter, is to promote and encourage respect for human rights and fundamental freedoms without distinction as to race, sex, language or religion. The Universal Declaration of Human Rights (UDHR) was

---

137. *See* Human Rights Council, *Report of the Working Group on the Universal Periodic Review: Ireland* (2011, A/HRC/19/9) para. 28 available at http://www.ohchr.org/Documents/HRBodies/HRCouncil/RegularSession/Session19/A-HRC-19-9_en.pdf (accessed 27 Aug. 2019).

138. The two main organs of the UN with responsibility for human rights are the Human Rights Council of which Ireland is a member and the Office of the High Commissioner for Human Rights.

adopted by the UN General Assembly in 1948 and achieved the goal of producing a non-binding Declaration. Combined with the International Covenant on Civil and Political Rights 1966 (ICCPR) and the International Covenant on Economic, Social and Cultural Rights 1966 (ICESCR), all three cumulatively provide a legally binding Convention and continue to represent the cornerstone of international human rights law.

69. As a member of the UN since 1955, Ireland is expected to uphold its principles and protect the rights set out in international treaties through its laws, policies and practices. To date, Ireland has ratified a number of UN human rights treaties, including the International Covenant on Civil and Political Rights (1966); the International Covenant on Economic, Social and Cultural Rights (1966); the Convention on the Elimination of All Forms of Racial Discrimination (1965); the Convention on the Elimination of All Forms of Discrimination against Women (1979); the Convention against Torture and Other Cruel, Inhuman or Degrading Treatment or Punishment (1984); the Convention on the Rights of the Child (1989); and the Convention on the Rights of Persons with Disabilities (2006). However, as noted above, the incorporation of international treaties and covenants is contingent on legislation. The extent to which each of these conventions has been given domestic effect varies.

§3. Key Provisions of the UDHR and ICCPR

70. The freedom of thought, conscience and religion is one of the UN's main fundamental rights, with key provisions found in Article 18 of both the UDHR 1948 and the ICCPR 1966. Article 18 of the UDHR states:

> Everyone has the right to freedom of thought, conscience and religion; this right includes freedom to change his religion or belief, and freedom, either alone or in community with others and in public or private, to manifest his religion or belief in teaching, practice, worship and observance.[139]

71. As Lindkvist explains, 'although it is clear that the Universal Declaration did not mark the first time the freedom of conscience received international recognition, it helped to redefine it as a freedom of the individual human person'.[140]

72. Article 18 of the ICCPR seeks to build upon the UDHR with its own freedom of religion clause. It states:

> 1. Everyone shall have the right to freedom of thought, conscience and religion. This right shall include freedom to have or to adopt a religion or

139. Article 18 is limited by Art. 29(2) which states: 'In the exercise of his rights and freedoms, everyone shall be subject only to such limitations as are determined by law solely for the purpose of securing due recognition and respect for the rights and freedoms of others and of meeting the just requirements of morality, public order and the general welfare in a democratic society.'
140. Linde Lindkvist, *Religious Freedom and the Universal Declaration of Human Rights* 21–60 (Cambridge University Press, 2017).

belief of his choice, and freedom, either individually or in community with others and in public or private, to manifest his religion or belief in worship, observance, practice and teaching.

2. No one shall be subject to coercion which would impair his freedom to have or to adopt a religion or belief of his choice.
3. Freedom to manifest one's religion or beliefs may be subject only to such limitations as are prescribed by law and are necessary to protect public safety, order, health, or morals or the fundamental rights and freedoms of others.
4. The States Parties to the present Covenant undertake to have respect for the liberty of parents and, when applicable, legal guardians to ensure the religious and moral education of their children in conformity with their own convictions.[141]

73. Article 26 of the Covenant further includes a general non-discrimination principle which also covers religion.[142]

§4. Ireland: An Analysis

74. UN treaties are enforced through supervision and reporting by expert bodies. In particular, the Universal Periodic Review, created in 2006, plays an important role.[143] A tool of the UN Human Rights Council, it is a state-driven process that sees the peer review of the human rights record of all UN Member States every four and a half years with regard to the human rights commitments each State made when ratifying various UN human rights treaties.[144]

75. Separately, the UN Human Rights Committee is a body of independent experts that seeks to monitor the implementation of the ICCPR by state parties.[145] All state parties must submit regular reports to the Committee on how the rights are being implemented. Initially, states must report one year after acceding to the Covenant and usually every four years thereafter or upon request by the Committee. The Committee examines the submitted report and outlines any concerns and recommendations to the state party in its 'concluding observations'. The Human Rights Committee is composed of eighteen independent experts, described as 'persons of high moral character and recognized competence in the field of human rights'.[146]

76. In its 2020 periodic report on Ireland (reflecting on the combined fifth to ninth reports produced on the jurisdiction), a number of concluding observations on

141. For more, *see* Linde Lindkvist, *Religious Freedom and the Universal Declaration of Human Rights* (Cambridge University Press, 2017).
142. Note, beyond the UDHR and the ICCPR, the principle of freedom of religion also appears in a number of other texts including in Art. 14 of the International Convention on the Rights of the Child.
143. *See*, https://www.ohchr.org/en/hrbodies/upr/pages/uprmain.aspx (accessed 9 Jun. 2023).
144. *See*, https://www.ohchr.org/en/hrbodies/upr/pages/uprmain.aspx (accessed 9 Jun. 2023).
145. *See*, https://www.ohchr.org/EN/HRBodies/CCPR/Pages/CCPRIntro.aspx (accessed 9 Jun. 2023).
146. *See*, https://www.ohchr.org/EN/HRBodies/CCPR/Pages/Membership.aspx (accessed 9 Jun. 2023). Members are elected for a term of four years under Arts 28–39 of the Covenant.

the State's performance in relation to freedom of religion were flagged by the UN Human Rights Committee.[147] First, the Committee noted its 'concern' vis-à-vis the 'reportedly high level of racist hate crime targeted at ethnic minorities, which is often in combination with other grounds of discrimination such as gender and religion'.[148] It highlighted its further concerns that the existing criminal laws did 'not include substantive racist hate crime offences or provide for aggravating circumstances for such a crime', noting, in addition, 'the absence of legislation that declares illegal and prohibits racist organizations in the light of the escalation in incidents of far-right rhetoric and racist hate crime targeted at ethnic minority groups'.[149] It therefore recommended that, among other measures, Ireland introduce a) 'legislative provisions that include racist motivation as an aggravating circumstance that will result in a penalty enhancement for crimes committed as a result of racial bias' and b) 'legislation to declare illegal and prohibit racist organizations in accordance with article 4 (b) of the Convention'.[150]

77. Second, having previously noted its 'concern' in relation to 'the slow progress in increasing access to secular education',[151] the Committee welcomed the enactment of the Education (Admission to Schools) Act 2018, removing a derogation which formerly applied to permit certain schools to use religion as a selection criterion.[152] Nevertheless, cognisant of the lack of information on the impact of this reform, the Committee recommended that Ireland provide such data going forward.[153]

---

147. Human Rights Committee, *Concluding observations on the combined fifth to ninth reports of Ireland* (2020, CERD/C/IRL/CO/5-9) available to download at https://www.ohchr.org/en/documents/concluding-observations/cerdcirlco5-9-committee-elimination-racial-discrimination (accessed 9 Jun. 2023).
148. Human Rights Committee, *Concluding observations on the combined fifth to ninth reports of Ireland* (2020, CERD/C/IRL/CO/5-9) para. 21 available to download at https://www.ohchr.org/en/documents/concluding-observations/cerdcirlco5-9-committee-elimination-racial-discrimination (accessed 9 Jun. 2023).
149. Human Rights Committee, *Concluding observations on the combined fifth to ninth reports of Ireland* (2020, CERD/C/IRL/CO/5-9) para. 21 available to download at https://www.ohchr.org/en/documents/concluding-observations/cerdcirlco5-9-committee-elimination-racial-discrimination (accessed 9 Jun. 2023).
150. Human Rights Committee, *Concluding observations on the combined fifth to ninth reports of Ireland* (2020, CERD/C/IRL/CO/5-9) para. 22 available to download at https://www.ohchr.org/en/documents/concluding-observations/cerdcirlco5-9-committee-elimination-racial-discrimination (accessed 9 Jun. 2023). In this regard, note the Criminal Justice (Incitement to Violence or Hatred and Hate Offences) Bill 2022 discussed further below.
151. Human Rights Committee, *Concluding Observations on the Fourth Periodic Report of Ireland* (2014, CCPR/C/IRL/CO/4) available to download at https://tbinternet.ohchr.org/_layouts/15/treatybodyexternal/Download.aspx?symbolno=CCPR/C/IRL/CO/4&Lang=En (accessed 27 Aug. 2019).
152. Human Rights Committee, *Concluding observations on the combined fifth to ninth reports of Ireland* (2020, CERD/C/IRL/CO/5-9) para. 29 available to download at https://www.ohchr.org/en/documents/concluding-observations/cerdcirlco5-9-committee-elimination-racial-discrimination (accessed 9 Jun. 2023). *See* Part IX for more.
153. Human Rights Committee, *Concluding observations on the combined fifth to ninth reports of Ireland* (2020, CERD/C/IRL/CO/5-9) para. 22 available to download at https://www.ohchr.org/en/documents/concluding-observations/cerdcirlco5-9-committee-elimination-racial-discrimination (accessed 9 Jun. 2023).

78. Previous reports had highlighted various other aspects of Irish law relating to religious freedom which were deemed to be of concern. In 2014, the Committee expressed its concern at 'the slow pace of progress in amending the provisions of the Constitution that oblige individuals wishing to take up senior public office positions … to take religious oaths'.[154] It recommended that Ireland 'should take concrete steps' to amend Articles 12, 31 and 34 of the Irish Constitution 'taking into account the committee's general comment No. 22 (1993) on freedom of thought, conscience and religion, concerning the right not to be compelled to reveal one's thoughts or adherence to a religion or belief in public'.[155] This call has been supported by others who note of the constitutional oath: 'This declaration is essentially a religious test for holding office as it discriminates against non-Christians and persons with non-religious beliefs, while also violating their rights to freedom of religion, freedom from religion and freedom of conscience.'[156]

79. The 2014 report also expressed 'further concern' that pursuant to section 37(1) of the Employment Equality Acts, religious-owned institutions, including in the fields of education and health, can discriminate against employees or prospective employees to protect the religious ethos of the institution.[157] This prompted a recommendation that section 37(1) of the Employment Equality Act ought to be amended 'in a way that bars all forms of discrimination in employment in the fields of education and health'.[158]

80. Although these recommendations remain outstanding, others put forward in the 2014 report were acted on in the intervening years. On the issue of blasphemy, the Committee noted that it remained 'concerned' that (as of 2014) it continued to be a constitutional and legislative offence under Article 40.6.1(i) of the Irish Constitution and section 36 of the Defamation Act 2009, respectively. Having noted that '[p]rohibitions of displays of lack of respect for a religion or other belief system, including blasphemy laws, are incompatible' with Article 19 of the ICCPR, which

154. Human Rights Committee, *Concluding Observations on the Fourth Periodic Report of Ireland* (2014, CCPR/C/IRL/CO/4) available to download at https://tbinternet.ohchr.org/_layouts/15/treatybodyexternal/Download.aspx?symbolno=CCPR/C/IRL/CO/4&Lang=En (accessed 27 Aug. 2019).

155. Human Rights Committee, *Concluding Observations on the Fourth Periodic Report of Ireland* (2014, CCPR/C/IRL/CO/4) available to download at https://tbinternet.ohchr.org/_layouts/15/treatybodyexternal/Download.aspx?symbolno=CCPR/C/IRL/CO/4&Lang=En (accessed 27 Aug. 2019).

156. Jamie McLoughlin, '"In the Presence of Almighty God": The Human Rights Violations at the Heart of the Irish Constitution' 35(17) *Irish Law Times* 230 (2017). He argues that 'the religious oath requirements and the blasphemy provision are inconsistent with well-established international human rights norms'. For more *see* Part VII Ch. 4.

157. Human Rights Committee, *Concluding Observations on the Fourth Periodic Report of Ireland* (2014, CCPR/C/IRL/CO/4) available to download at https://tbinternet.ohchr.org/_layouts/15/treatybodyexternal/Download.aspx?symbolno=CCPR/C/IRL/CO/4&Lang=En (accessed 27 Aug. 2019).

158. Human Rights Committee, *Concluding Observations on the Fourth Periodic Report of Ireland* (2014, CCPR/C/IRL/CO/4) available to download at https://tbinternet.ohchr.org/_layouts/15/treatybodyexternal/Download.aspx?symbolno=CCPR/C/IRL/CO/4&Lang=En (accessed 27 Aug. 2019). *See* Part VII Ch. 7 below for more on recent developments in this area.

guarantees freedom of expression and with Article 26, which secures non-discrimination in the enjoyment of Covenant Rights,[159] the Committee recommended reform.[160] These proposals were accepted in 2018 with both the constitutional and legislative provisions regarding blasphemy removed from Irish law.[161]

159. UN Human Rights Committee, *General Comment No. 34, Article 19, Freedoms of Opinion and Expression* (2011, CCPR/C/GC/34) available at http://www.refworld.org/docid/4ed34b562.html (accessed 27 Aug. 2019).

160. UN Human Rights Committee, *General Comment No. 34, Article 19, Freedoms of Opinion and Expression* (2011, CCPR/C/GC/34) available at http://www.refworld.org/docid/4ed34b562.html (accessed 27 Aug. 2019). For recent developments in relation to blasphemy, *see* Part VII Ch. 3.

161. *See* Part VII, Ch. 3 for more.

Chapter 2. Transnational Law Effects on Religious Communities

§1. European Convention on Human Rights

81. The European Convention for the Protection of Human Rights and Fundamental Freedoms, more widely known as the European Convention on Human Rights (ECHR), continues to provide the basis for the European human rights system. First drafted by the Council of Europe in 1950, it has been in force since 1953. Ireland ratified the ECHR in 1953.

82. Where an individual believes his/her Convention rights have been breached, he/she must first exhaust the legal remedies at a domestic level. If their claim has not been upheld at a national level, they may make an application to the European Court of Human Rights (ECtHR). Notwithstanding that it was established specifically to secure compliance with the Convention by state governments, the ECtHR ensures a margin of appreciation that allows states to differ from each other in relation to their laws and policies to facilitate different cultures and needs.

83. The Court may be petitioned by a person, a non-governmental organisation or a group of individuals so long as the applicant is a victim of a violation of one of the rights enshrined in the Convention. Moreover, the alleged violation must be by one or more state signatories, a governmental organisation or a person acting as an official of the state. In 2022, the Court dealt with twenty-eight applications concerning Ireland.[162] Of these, although twenty-seven were declared inadmissible or struck out, the Court delivered one judgment (concerning one application), which found no violation of the ECHR.

84. Convention rights may be exercised by churches and other religious bodies. Although it has been noted that at a technical level, such groups are exercising the individual rights of their members,[163] provided that the body is non-governmental,[164] such religious bodies are 'capable of possessing and exercising the rights … in its own capacity as a representative of its members'.[165]

85. Despite the fact that Ireland was one of the original countries that first signed the ECHR, it was slow to legislate to give it domestic effect. Developments in Northern Ireland, specifically the signing of the Good Friday/Belfast Agreement in 1998, however, brought the issue to the fore, requiring the Irish Government to commit to introducing the Convention into domestic law.[166] Today, the ECHR Act

162. Press Unit of the European Court of Human Rights, *Press Country Profile* (2023) available at https://www.echr.coe.int/Documents/CP_Ireland_ENG.pdf (accessed 9 Jun. 2023).
163. *See* Russell Sandberg, 'Religion and the Individual: A Socio-Legal Perspective' in Abby Day (ed.) *Religion and the Individual* 157–169 (Ashgate, 2008).
164. *Holy Monasteries v. Greece* (1995) 20 EHRR 1.
165. *X and the Church of Scientology v. Sweden* (1979) 16 DR 68.
166. *See* Donncha O'Connell, 'The Added Value of Sub-constitutional Incorporation: ECHR Act 2003' in Eoin Carolan & Oran Doyle (eds) *The Irish Constitution: Governance and Values* 490 (Roundhall, 2008).

2003 ensures that the standards set out in the ECHR have an effect on domestic law. As a result, these rights may be considered before the Irish courts.[167] It is important to bear in mind, however, that where there is any uncertainty, the Irish Constitution retains primacy over the 2003 Act, and in the event of a conflict between the two, it is the Constitution that will prevail.

86. Notwithstanding this, by virtue of the ECHR Act 2003, Convention rights, including the freedom of religion under Article 9, are now part of domestic law and are justiciable in domestic courts. Article 9 of the Convention provides:

1. Everyone has the right to freedom of thought, conscience and religion; this right includes freedom to change his religion or belief and freedom, either alone or in community with others and in public or private, to manifest his religion or belief, in worship, teaching, practice and observance.
2. Freedom to manifest one's religion or beliefs shall be subject only to such limitations as are prescribed by law and are necessary in a democratic society in the interests of public safety, for the protection of public order, health or morals, or for the protection of the rights and freedoms of others.[168]

87. Thus, the freedom of thought, conscience and religion is absolute with a positive obligation placed on the state to allow individuals the right to manifest and enjoy their beliefs peacefully and without undue interference.[169]

88. The ECtHR has produced a Guide on Article 9 of the ECHR.[170] Reflecting on the importance of Article 9, it states:

> Freedom of thought, conscience and religion as enshrined in Article 9 of the Convention represents one of the foundations of a 'democratic society' within the meaning of the Convention. It is, in its religious dimension, one of the most vital elements that go to make up the identity of believers and their conception of life, but it is also a precious asset for atheists, agnostics, sceptics and the unconcerned.[171]

89. However, as evident in Article 9(2), the freedom to 'manifest' religious rites or beliefs is limited, and the courts have allowed states a generous margin of

167. The Act now empowers the Irish courts to issue a declaration of incompatibility in cases where they find a provision of Irish law to be inconsistent with the Convention, *see* Jamie McLoughlin, '"In the presence of Almighty God": The Human Rights Violations at the Heart of the Irish Constitution' 35(17) *Irish Law Times* 230 (2017).
168. *See also* Art. 14 of the Convention which prohibits discrimination based on various grounds including religion and opinions.
169. *See Lachiri v. Belgium* (2018) (Application No. 3413/09).
170. European Court of Human Rights, *Guide on Article 9 of the European Convention on Human Rights* (Updated on 31 Dec. 2018) available at https://www.echr.coe.int/Documents/Guide_Art_9_ENG.pdf (accessed 27 Aug. 2019).
171. European Court of Human Rights, Guide on Art. 9 of the ECHR (Updated on 31 Dec. 2018) 7–8 available at https://www.echr.coe.int/Documents/Guide_Art_9_ENG.pdf (accessed 27 Aug. 2019).

appreciation in balancing religious rights with other rights or social interests.[172] Whether this approach (which often sees the rights of the majority prevail) adequately protects the religious and other views of minority groups is questionable.[173] It has been suggested that Article 9 has been 'of limited use to claimants'.[174]

§2. The European Union

90. Although initially focused on economic affairs, the development of the European Union (EU) over recent decades, in particular, has resulted in an expansion in the amount of its laws and regulatory instruments concerned with religion. In this context, it has been noted that today scholars are increasingly talking about 'EU law on religion' as a distinct legal category.[175] Doe suggests that the 'contemporary posture' of the EU vis-à-vis religion is founded on seven fundamentals which are summed up in the Lisbon Treaty 2007: the value of religion; subsidiarity; religious freedom; religious equality (and non-discrimination); the autonomy of religious associations; cooperation with religion (through frequent dialogue); and the special protection of religion by means of privileges and exemptions.[176]

91. Since acceding to the then European Communities in 1972, the treaties and laws of the EU are now incorporated into the domestic law of Ireland. As EU law has expanded to involve issues of religion, there has been a knock-on effect on religion law in Ireland. For example, Regulation 4 of Council Regulation (EC) No. 1099/2009 of 24 September 2009 on the protection of animals at the time of killing provides that rules regulating the stunning methods used in the slaughter of animals do not apply in the case of animals subject to particular methods of slaughter prescribed by religious rites provided that the slaughter takes place in a slaughterhouse. This Regulation has now been transposed into Irish law through the EU (Protection of Animals at the Time of Killing) Regulations 2013. Consequently, although the issue appears to be generating increasing controversy,[177] ritual slaughter remains possible in Ireland pursuant to the Animal, Health and Welfare Act 2013.

---

172. *See*, for example, *Dahlab v. Switzerland* (2001) (Application No. 42393/98). Note, Irish case law on Art. 9 established that it does not secure the right to divorce. *See Johnston and Others v. Ireland* (1986) (Application No. 9697/82). However, divorce was introduced in Ireland in 1996 following a referendum. *See* Part X for more.
173. *See* Jilan Kamal, 'Justified Interference with Religious Freedom: The European Court of Human Rights and the Need for Mediating Doctrine under Article 9(2)' 46 *Columbia Journal of Transnational Law* 667 (2008); M. Todd Parker, 'The Freedom to Manifest Religious Belief: An Analysis of the Necessity Clauses of the ICCPR and the ECHR' 17 *Duke Journal of Comparative & International Law* 91 (2006).
174. Megan Pearson, 'Article 9 at a Crossroads: Interference Before and After Eweida' 13(3) *Human Rights Law Review* 580, 580 (2013).
175. Norman Doe, 'Towards a "Common Law" on Religion in the European Union' 37 *Journal of Religion, State and Society* 147 (2009).
176. *See* Norman Doe, *Law and Religion in Europe: A Comparative Introduction* Ch. 10 (OUP, 2011).
177. *See*, for example, Noel Bardon, 'Vets want tightening of slaughter stunning rules', *Irish Farmer's Journal*, 7 Dec. 2022. For early Irish legislation in this area, *see* the Slaughter of Animals Act 1935.

Recent EU initiatives in relation to privacy law have also had a significant impact. EU General Data Protection Regulation (GDPR) prompted the introduction of the Data Protection Act 2018, effecting significant changes to the data protection framework in Ireland, which was previously established under the Data Protection Acts 1988 and 2003. The impact that these changes have had on religious organisations will be considered further in Part VII Chapter 1.

Chapter 3. Regional Law Effects on Religious Communities

92. There are no regional laws in Ireland that have an effect on religious communities.

Part V. Religion and Politics

Introduction

93. To date, there has been relatively little effort made to increase the legal regulation of religious groups or individuals in Ireland. In fact, some religious leaders have called for greater regulation – particularly within the Muslim community – as a means of preventing extremism.[178] Nevertheless, with ever-increasing multiculturalism (and also driven by international pressures), the links between faith, religion and social cohesion have gained increased prominence in the jurisdiction.[179] This part will consider some of the initiatives and structures formed by the Irish State to encourage dialogue with and support religious groups. It will then turn to consider the initiatives and structures formed by religious groups to promote dialogue amongst themselves as well as with state bodies and institutions/structures before briefly considering the interaction between religion and the Irish State on a political and legal level.

178. *See* the comments of Shaykh Dr Umar Al-Qadri, Chairman of the Irish Muslim Peace and Integration Council as quoted in Abigail Frymann Rouch, 'Regulate All Mosques to Stop Radical Preachers: Irish Imam' *Irish Independent*, 19 Dec. 2016. *See also* Cormac O'Keefe, 'Government Should Regulate Mosques and Do Checks, Says Imam Ibrahim Noonan' *Irish Examiner*, 31 Jul. 2016. *See* further James Carr & Bryan Fanning, 'Muslim Dilemmas in the Republic of Ireland: Anti-Extremism and Self-Regulation in the Context of Super-Diversity' (2019) 30(2) *Islam and Christian–Muslim Relations* 149–163.

179. *See* Norman Doe, *Law and Religion in Europe: A Comparative Introduction* (OUP, 2011). *See also*, Directorate-General for Parliamentary Research Services (European Parliament), *Religion and the EU's External Policies* (2017) available at https://publications.europa.eu/en/publication-detail/-/publication/acc8079e-e603-11e7-9749-01aa75ed71a1 (accessed 27 Aug. 2019).

Chapter 1. Religion Influence on Politics

§1. Governmental Responsibilities

94. Since, in particular, the mid-1990s, Ireland has become ever more multicultural. Cognisant of these social shifts, the first significant Government publication vis-à-vis integration policy in the jurisdiction was published in 1999, entitled 'Integration: A two-way process'.[180] Produced by the Interdepartmental Working Group on the Integration of Refugees in Ireland for the Minister for Justice, Equality and Law Reform, the report focused on the need to identify and remove barriers or impediments to the integration of asylum seekers and other foreign nationals. While not focused on religion, specifically, the document was an initial attempt to place the spotlight on the needs of people from different backgrounds and cultures.

95. Although in April 2000, the Commissioner of An Garda Síochána (the national police service of Ireland) established the Garda Racial, Intercultural & Diversity Office, it was not until June 2007 that the Office of the Minister for Integration was established within the Irish Department of Justice. Soon after, the first Ministerial statement on the issue of integration was produced with the publication of 'Migration Nation: A Statement on Integration Strategy and Diversity Management'.[181] In developing integration policy (whether for religious minorities or otherwise), it sought to emphasise the need for whole-of-government and localised community-level approaches. In seeking to avoid the emergence of segregated community identities, it highlighted the importance of community partnerships and inclusive service delivery.

96. The Office of the Minister for Integration was subsequently renamed the Office for the Promotion of Migrant Integration in 2011. In 2020, responsibility for policy concerning migrant integration was transferred to the Department of Children, Equality, Disability, Integration and Youth. Despite not directly referencing religion, one of its key functions is tackling racism and discrimination,[182] with the Office having explicitly noted the responsiveness of faith-based groups 'to the arrival of migrants to Ireland in terms of providing support, assistance and information'.[183] It continues to develop, lead and coordinate migrant integration policy across Government departments, agencies and services and, in 2017, published 'The Migrant Integration Strategy: A blueprint for the future'.[184] Soon after, in March 2018, the Office published a 'Review Report on Promoting Political Engagement of Migrants' with a particular focus on encouraging participation in the 2019 Local

180. 'Integration: A two-way process' available at https://migrant-integration.ec.europa.eu/library-document/integration-two-way-process-1_en (accessed 29 Feb. 2024).
181. Available at, https://migrant-integration.ec.europa.eu/library-document/migration-nation-statement-integration-strategy-and-diversity-management_en (accessed 29 Feb. 2024).
182. *See*, https://www.gov.ie/en/publication/983af-migrant-integration-strategy/ (accessed 9 Jun. 2023).
183. *See*, http://www.integration.ie/en/ISEC/Pages/Mig_Info_Making_Friends (accessed 9 Jun. 2023).
184. For 'The Migrant Integration Strategy: A blueprint for the future', *see*, https://www.gov.ie/en/publication/983af-migrant-integration-strategy/ (accessed 29 Feb. 2024).

Elections,[185] while in June 2019, a progress report on the Migrant Integration Strategy was presented to the government.[186] The Office for the Promotion of Migrant Integration also oversees the Communities Integration Fund with a total fund of over EUR 500,000 available to support community integration projects.[187]

97. It is worthwhile to note, however, that although Government integration policy has expanded from its initial focus on asylum seekers to now include all legally resident non-Irish nationals – and does implicitly encourage respect for religious pluralism – the integration of non-migrant Irish nationals from different religious or ethnic backgrounds appears to remain largely overlooked. This is particularly notable given the findings of Census 2022 which found that 54% of those who identified as Muslim and 25% of those who identified as Hindu were Irish citizens.[188]

98. Finally, the provision for a Church-State Structured Dialogue Process, effectively a more formalised dialogue between the political institutions of the State (primarily the Department of An Taoiseach) and religious bodies, was established in early 2007.[189] While the extent to which this process was relied upon was somewhat unclear, in 2019, then Taoiseach Leo Varadkar suggested a desire within the Government to establish a new 'covenant' between the Church and State.[190] It was

185. *See*, https://www.gov.ie/en/speech/e93da2-speech-by-mr-david-stanton-td-at-promoting-political-engagement-of-m/ (accessed 9 Jun. 2023).
186. *See*, https://www.gov.ie/en/publication/983af-migrant-integration-strategy/ (accessed 9 Jun. 2023).
187. In 2023, a number of faith-based groups were successful in securing funding for such projects, *see*, https://www.gov.ie/en/press-release/c3195-minister-joe-obrien-announces-111-projects-to-be-funded-under-the-communities-integration-fund-2023/ (accessed 9 Jun. 2023). Note also the National Integration Fund, see https://www.gov.ie/en/press-release/b401d-minister-of-state-obrien-invites-applications-to-the-national-integration-fund-2023/ (accessed 29 Feb. 2024).
188. *See*, https://www.cso.ie/en/releasesandpublications/ep/p-cpsr/censusofpopulation2022-summaryresults/migrationanddiversity/ (accessed 9 Jun. 2023).
189. *See*, https://www.oireachtas.ie/en/debates/question/2007-04-25/3/ (accessed 17 Jan. 2021). *See also* Kenneth Houston, 'Formalised Church-State Dialogue in Ireland: A Critique of Concept' 3(1) *Irish Journal of Public Policy* (2009). Note, Art. 16C of the Lisbon Treaty commits EU Member States to 'open, regular and transparent' dialogue with religious associations and non-confessional bodies.
190. *See*, https://www.oireachtas.ie/en/debates/question/2019-05-21/6/ (accessed 27 Aug. 2019). In initially announcing the proposed structured dialogue process in 2004, the then *Taoiseach* Bertie Ahern noted: 'The views being sought on the proposed structured dialogue are those of the Roman Catholic Church, the Church of Ireland, the Presbyterian Church, the Methodist Church, the Religious Society of Friends, the Salvation Army, the Unitarian Church, the Lutheran Church of Ireland, the Moravian Church, the Baptist Church, the Orthodox Church, which is the Coptic, Greek, Romanian and Russian Church, the Church of Jesus Christ of Latter-Day Saints, Jehovah's Witnesses, the Jewish community, the Islamic Foundation of Ireland, the Baha'i Faith, the Buddhist centres and the Association of Irish Humanists. We are happy to engage with other churches and faith communities that may wish to be involved – I hope there are not 130 of them.' *See*, https://www.oireachtas.ie/ga/debates/question/2004-12-14/2/. In the more recent discussion however, *Taoiseach* Varadkar took a less prescriptive approach and noted that the process would involve planned dialogue between the State and churches, philosophical and non-confessional organisations in Ireland. This would appear to be a more practical approach given the large number of religious bodies

highlighted by An Taoiseach that it would mark the beginning of 'a new relationship that is more about pluralism than about absolute secularism'.[191] A plenary meeting with members of the Government and representatives of almost thirty different churches, faith communities and non-confessional organisations took place on 4 July 2019 in Dublin Castle and was described as an 'important consultative step in developing the relationship between Church and State'.[192] However, little progress appears to have been made in the interim with consultations between the state and religious organisations typically following a more informal format.

§2. The Irish Human Rights and Equality Commission

99. The IHREC is an independent public body and operates as Ireland's national human rights and equality institution.[193] The Commission accounts to the Oireachtas (the Irish legislature) and enjoys a mandate established under the IHREC Act 2014. The Commission is made up of fifteen members appointed by the President of Ireland. The Commission notes its purpose is 'to protect and promote human rights and equality in Ireland and build a culture of respect for human rights, equality and intercultural understanding in the State'.[194] Pursuant to section 10(1) of the IHREC Act 2014, the functions of the Commission include protecting and promoting human rights and equality; encouraging the development of a culture of respect for human rights, equality, and intercultural understanding in the State; encouraging good practice in intercultural relations; and promoting tolerance and acceptance of diversity in the State and respect for the freedom and dignity of each person. At the level of policy, the Commission is tasked with reviewing the effectiveness of human rights and equality law, policy and practice in the State and within public bodies. It is also empowered to provide practical help, including legal assistance, to aid people in defending their rights and may contribute to legal cases (as amicus curiae) that deal with an individual's equality or human rights concerns.

§3. The Charities Regulatory Authority

100. Unsurprisingly, a large number of faith-based or religious-based organisations are represented on the public Register of Charities in Ireland, usually for the

afforded legislative recognition under the Civil Registration Act 2004 (for the solemnisation of marriage), *see* Susan Leahy & Kathryn O'Sullivan, 'Changing Conceptions of Marriage in Ireland: Law and Practice' 30(3) *Child and Family Law Quarterly* 279 (2018).

191. *See* https://www.oireachtas.ie/en/debates/question/2019-05-21/6/ (accessed 27 Aug. 2019).

192. *See* https://www.gov.ie/en/press-release/9374bc-church-state-dialogue-plenary-meeting-with-churches-faith-communitie/ (accessed 17 Jan. 2021).

193. *See* https://www.ihrec.ie/about/who-we-are/ (accessed 9 Jun. 2023). It is the successor body to the Irish Human Rights Commission.

194. *See* https://www.ihrec.ie/about/who-we-are/ (accessed 9 Jun. 2023).

purpose of the 'advancement of religion'.[195] As a result, the Charities Regulatory Authority plays an increasingly important role in the regulation of religious or faith-based organisations in the jurisdiction.[196]

101. Established in 2014 under the Charities Act 2009 (as amended), the Charities Regulator is an independent authority and acts as Ireland's national statutory regulator for charitable organisations. Among its key functions is establishing and maintaining the Charities Register and ensuring the compliance of charities with the Charities Acts. All organisations on the Register are compelled to provide information to the Charities Regulatory Authority on their activities on a yearly basis; however, the level of oversight to which they are subject depends on the gross income of the charity in question. While the Authority does address the issue of 'the advancement of religion' in its What is a Charity Guidelines,[197] no specific guidelines on the topic have been produced to date. Moreover, no clear or explicit support in the form of workshops or other for religious or faith-based charities appears to have been provided thus far in Ireland.

195. Section 3 of the Charities Act 2009 (as amended). For the Register of Charities, *see* https://www.charitiesregulator.ie/en/information-for-the-public/search-the-register-of-charities (accessed 9 Jun. 2023).
196. *See* above Part III Ch. 1 for more on the law regulating charities in Ireland.
197. https://www.charitiesregulator.ie/media/1544/what-is-a-charity-rev-001.pdf (accessed 9 Jun. 2023).

Chapter 2. Political Influence in Religion

102. In addition to the institutions and structures put in place by the Irish State to engage with and (directly or indirectly) support religious or faith-based groups, religious groups themselves have also established organisations to facilitate dialogue both *inter partes* and with the Irish State.[198] It is to these religious groups or bodies that we must now turn.

§1. ASSOCIATION OF LEADERS OF MISSIONARIES AND RELIGIOUS OF IRELAND

103. The Association of Leaders of Missionaries and Religious of Ireland (AMRI) was established in 2016 arising from the amalgamation of the Irish Missionary Union and the Conference of Religious of Ireland. Based at Cypress Grove in Dublin, its Memorandum of Association notes its main object is 'the advancement of religion through the provision of a forum for consultation and co-operation between Catholic religious institutes, societies of apostolic life and missionaries and to provide support and promote the common interests of the member organisations in Ireland'.[199] It states 'Mission and Dialogue' as one of its strategic goals, promoting collaboration 'by engaging with existing and emerging realities in the Church and wider society'.[200] In its Strategic Plan 2018–2021, it notes it will '[f]oster mission and dialogue with the Irish Episcopal Conference (IEC), relevant Church bodies and associated agencies' as well as extend 'the hand of friendship and communion through its promotion of inter-religious and inter-cultural dialogue'.[201]

§2. ISLAMIC CULTURAL CENTRE OF IRELAND

104. Having regard to the level of state visits undertaken by official representatives of the Irish Government (including the Taoiseach and President) to the Clonskeagh headquarters of the Islamic Cultural Centre of Ireland (ICCI), it has been observed that it is there 'to which official Ireland turns when it wishes to acknowledge and/or welcome the State's growing Muslim community'.[202] As a result, although a number of other independent mosque associations reject the claims of the ICCI to represent all Muslims in the State,[203] it does play an important role in

---

198. While these organisations will have not greater legal standing than any individual religious organisation, per se, they can have a greater legal and political influence by virtue of their broader membership. Most are registered charities.
199. *See* https://docs.wixstatic.com/ugd/cacca5_0fa0300c6027455683a7dc4a3c61db57.pdf (accessed 9 Jun. 2023).
200. *See* https://www.amri.ie/ (accessed 9 Jun. 2023).
201. *See* https://docs.wixstatic.com/ugd/cacca5_1646bfe0570e4930be436d5d592457a0.pdf (accessed 9 Jun. 2023).
202. Patsy McGarry, 'Centre in Clonskeagh Is Major Symbol of Islam in Ireland' *Irish Times*, 12 Mar. 2018. *See* https://islamireland.ie/ (accessed 9 Jun. 2023).
203. *See* Oliver Scharbrodt, 'Introduction' in Oliver Scharbrodt et al. (eds) *Muslims Past and Present* 15 (Edinburgh University Press, 2015); Adil Hussain Khan, Oliver Scharbrodt & Tuula Sakaranaho,

representing the Muslim community in Ireland. Incorporating a number of different mosques in Dublin and across the country, the ICCI also convenes the Irish Council of Imams. It notes its goal as preserving Islamic identity 'as well as encouraging the positive integration of Muslims, both Irish and Non-Irish, into the inter-cultural society we now live in'.[204]

§3. Irish Muslim Peace & Integration Council

105. The Irish Muslim Peace & Integration Council is another national body representing the Muslim community in Ireland and appears to be growing in importance with a presence now established in Dublin, Cork, Athlone, Portlaoise and Belfast. Founded by Shaykh Dr Umar Al-Qadri, it is an independent body 'established to provide a forum where the Irish Muslim Community can speak as one recognised voice on matters relating to their well-being in Ireland, and help promote ways of integrating effectively in the community and promote the true teachings of Islam'.[205] Among its aims, the Irish Muslim Peace & Integration Council seeks to liaise with Government bodies and non-governmental organisations on matters concerning the Muslim community and to foster better community relations, promoting social inclusion, active citizenship and equality.[206] In terms of its objectives, the Irish Muslim Peace & Integration Council seeks to act 'as a voice for the Irish Muslims so as to enable them to highlight both to Development Boards and to other relevant agencies the issues affecting the delivery of services within the County [sic] for the Muslim community'.[207] It also seeks to influence the policies, strategies and overall decision-making process of relevant agencies in Ireland. Acting as a conduit for information and feedback to and from its network in relation to specific policies and initiatives, it strives to ensure that the concerns of the Muslim community are heard at a local and national level.

§4. The Irish Council of Churches

106. The Irish Council of Churches was founded in 1923 in the aftermath of the civil war and acts as the formal national body through which member churches formally engage, dialogue and act on a wide variety of issues.[208] Member Christian churches include Protestant, Orthodox, Reformed, Catholic, independent and migrant-led churches. Funding for the Council is derived from member churches. Relative to other such organisations, the Council appears particularly active in

---

'Mosque Communities and Muslim Organisation in Dublin and Other Cities' in Oliver Scharbrodt et al. (eds) *Muslims Past and Present* 113–128 (Edinburgh University Press, 2015). *See also* the comments of young respondents, for example, in Patsy McGarry, 'What Is It Like to Grow up Muslim in Ireland?' *Irish Times*, 28 Jan. 2017.

204. *See* https://islamireland.ie/about/about-icci/ (accessed 27 Aug. 2019).

205. *See* http://impic.ie/about-us (accessed 9 Jun. 2023).

206. *See* http://impic.ie/aims-and-objectives (accessed 9 Jun. 2023).

207. *See* http://impic.ie/aims-and-objectives (accessed 9 Jun. 2023).

208. *See* https://www.irishchurches.org/ (accessed 9 Jun. 2023).

facilitating discussion with political leaders both north and south of the border in Ireland and in acting as a liaison between the various churches and the Irish State. Moreover, in 2013, the European Affairs Committee of the Irish Council of Churches was established. Among its objectives is to bring 'a Christian judgement to bear on European Affairs', to help 'inform and share developments in European Affairs with the Irish churches' and to assist the Irish Council of Churches 'in developing policies, submissions and advocating on relevant aspects of European Affairs'.[209]

107. The Irish Council of Churches is also an associate member of Churches Together in Britain and Ireland, the successor to the former Council of Churches for Britain and Ireland and, before that, the British Council of Churches.[210] Linking the churches to a wide range of inter-church organisations, Churches Together in Britain and Ireland also arranges regular meetings of church representatives and facilitates dialogue between churches in England, Ireland, Scotland and Wales.

§5. Dublin City Interfaith Forum

108. The Dublin City Interfaith Forum (DCIF) was born out of the Irish Council of Churches' desire to engage with other faiths and initially represented a partnership between the Irish Council of Churches and Dublin City Council, supported by the European Investment Fund.[211] Today, members of the DCIF include representatives of various religious or faith-based organisations, including the Roman Catholic Church, the Church of Ireland, the Presbyterian Church, the Indian Orthodox Church as well as the Bahá'í, Buddhist, Jewish, Hindu, Sikh and Muslim communities. The Forum seeks to provide the space and opportunity for faith communities to build relationships with and between Dublin City communities, statutory and voluntary organisations and the residents of Dublin City.

209. *See* https://www.irishchurches.org/about/european-affairs-committee (accessed 9 Jun. 2023).
210. *See* https://ctbi.org.uk/ (accessed 9 Jun. 2023).
211. *See* https://www.irishchurches.org/about/dublin-city-interfaith-forum (accessed 27 Aug. 2019).

Chapter 3. Interaction Between Religion and State on a Political and Legal Level

§1. Historical Interaction in Ireland

109. Much has been written about the historical interaction between religion and the Irish State on a political and legal level. The political and cultural influence of the Roman Catholic Church, in particular, has attracted considerable academic attention. As Puirséil notes: 'The impact of the Roman Catholic Church on Irish politics has been immense ever since the early nineteenth century when clerical engagement and popular mobilization spurred the campaign for Catholic emancipation to victory.'[212] During this time, Fuller explains, 'the Catholic Church placed its resources and organizational ability at the disposal of Charles Stewart Parnell and Daniel O'Connell before him, and in so doing, had become a powerful political force destined to wield extraordinary influence in the new Irish state'.[213]

110. Throughout the twentieth century, religious identity, specifically Roman Catholic identity, became inextricably linked with national identity.[214] Notwithstanding that the relationship with the Roman Catholic Church was not formalised in the new Irish state (as an established church or other), it continued to play a powerful role in matters of state policy.[215] Indeed, reflecting on the important role held by W. T. Cosgrave and Eamon de Valera in ensuring that 'the Catholic moral code was upheld by legislation', Fuller notes the 'high point' of such influence came with the introduction of the 1937 Irish Constitution, Bunreacht na hÉireann.[216]

111. The first meaningful Church-State confrontation in post-Independence Ireland was arguably Noel Browne's infamous 'Mother and Child Scheme' in the early 1950s. It is broadly recognised that 'the controversy and the aftermath marked a crossroads in Irish Catholic culture, and the widening of a sub-culture of dissent which generally speaking had only involved the intelligentsia or literati up to that

212. Niamh Puirséil, 'Catholic Stakhanovites? Religion and the Irish Labour Party' in Francis Devine, Fintan Lane & Niamh Puirseil (eds) *Essays in Irish Labour History: A Festschrift for Elizabeth and John W. Boyle* 178 (Irish Academic Press, 2008). *See also* Kevin Costello & Niamh Howlin (eds) *Law and Religion in Ireland, 1700–1970* (Palgrave MacMillan, 2021).

213. Louise Fuller, 'Religion, Politics and Socio-Cultural Change in Twentieth Century Ireland' 10(1) *The European Legacy* 41, 41 (2005).

214. *See* John Coakley, 'Religion, National Identity and Political Change in Modern Ireland' 17(1) *Irish Political Studies* 4–28 (2002).

215. *See* Part III Ch. 1 for more. Eoin Daly, *Religion, Law and the Irish State* 5 (Clarus, 2012) suggests that the formalisation of the Church-State relationship was arguably viewed as unnecessary given its utter dominance.

216. Louise Fuller, 'Religion, Politics and Socio-Cultural Change in Twentieth Century Ireland' 10(1) *The European Legacy* 41, 41 (2005). *See* further Gerard Hogan, 'Legal Aspects of Church/State Relations In Ireland' (1988) 7 *St. Louis University Public Law Review* 275; Gerard Whyte, 'Religion and the Irish Constitution' (1996–1997) 30 *John Marshall Law Review* 725; Gerard Hogan, 'De Valera, The Constitution, and the Historians' (2006) 40 *Irish Jurist* 293.

time'.[217] Through subsequent decades, more liberal influences began to rise in Irish society, gathering particular momentum in the 1980s, 1990s and 2000s with an ever more secular agenda dominating Irish policy-making. The impact of these shifts will be discussed in greater detail throughout this monograph.[218]

§2. Representation in the Irish Parliament

112. There are no reserved positions within Oireachtas Éireann (the Irish Parliament) for representatives of religious bodies. Nevertheless, like many common law jurisdictions, a sitting of Dáil Éireann (the Lower House of the Irish Parliament) cannot commence without a prayer being read.[219] Pursuant to the current Dáil standing orders, a prayer is recited in both Irish and English at the beginning of each day's proceedings by the Ceann Comhairle (Chairperson). Since May 2017, TDs (Members of Parliament) have followed the daily prayer with a thirty-second silent reflection each day.[220] Similarly, in Seanad Éireann (the Senate), Standing Order 18 provides an identical prayer, which is recited, albeit that the silent reflection precedes the prayer in the Upper House:

> At the commencement of each sitting of the Seanad all Senators present shall stand for 30 seconds of silent reflection and then the following Prayer shall be read by the Clerk in the Irish and English languages: –
> Direct, we beseech Thee, O Lord, our actions by Thy holy inspirations and carry them on by Thy gracious assistance; that every word and work of ours may always begin from Thee, and by Thee be happily ended; through Christ Our Lord, Amen.[221]

---

217. Louise Fuller, 'Religion, Politics and Socio-Cultural Change in Twentieth Century Ireland' 10(1) *The European Legacy* 41, 47 (2005). She notes 'The Irish Times set the tone of the debate, when the morning after Browne's resignation the lead writer observed that "the Roman Catholic church would seem to be the effective government of the country."'

218. *See* James P MacKey & Enda McDonough (eds), *Religion and Politics in Ireland at the Turn of the Millennium: Essays in Honour of Garret FitzGerald on the Occasion of His Seventy-Fifth Birthday* (Columbia Press, 2004). Note, for example, the introduction by popular vote of divorce in 1996 and same-sex marriage in 2015. More recently, 2018 saw the removal of the 8th Amendment of the Constitution to facilitate the introduction of abortion in Ireland and the removal of the offence of publishing or uttering blasphemous matter as originally prohibited in Art. 40.6.1°. These issues will be considered in particular in Parts VII, X and XI.

219. A prayer or period of reflection is also applied in the parliaments of Australia, Canada, South Africa and the US.

220. *See* Standing Orders Relative to Public Business (2016), Order 27(1). Interestingly, a proposal in 2017 to abolish any prayer being said was heavily defeated, *see* https://www.rte.ie/news/politics/2017/0504/872523-dail-prayer/ (accessed 9 Jun. 2023).

221. *See* Standing Orders Relative to Public Business (2017), Order 18. Note, the period of reflection was only included in 2012 amendments to the Standing Orders.

Part VI. Labour Law Within Religious Communities

Introduction

113. This part considers the employment status of ministers of religion under Irish law – an issue which has generated little academic engagement or jurisprudence to date in the jurisdiction. It will highlight the general scope of the application of labour law before considering the position of ministers of religion vis-à-vis their working and social protection status. New procedural changes with regard to permission to work in Ireland as a minister for religion will be outlined before the position of other church employees and labour law is addressed.

Chapter 1. Scope of Application of Labour Law

114. Employees in Ireland enjoy various employment-related rights: from legislative provisions governing the minimum wage to those governing the maximum working week; from legislation regulating statutory protective leave (including maternity leave, paternity leave, adoptive leave, parental leave and carer's leave) to those regulating certain entitlements on redundancy. Due to the Unfair Dismissals Act 1977 (as amended), employees also enjoy relatively strong protection under Irish law against unfair dismissal, while a large body of common law has emerged to protect employees from wrongful dismissal.[222] The Employment Equality Act 1998 (as amended), meanwhile, plays a very important role in promoting equality and preventing discrimination in the context of employment.[223]

115. However, only those enjoying 'employee' status can benefit from such employment-related rights. In order to determine whether a worker is an employee with a contract of service or is self-employed with a contract for services (e.g., as an independent contractor), the courts have long struggled to set out a definitive test.[224] A so-called Control Test initially found favour with the courts. Although it sought to determine and place a premium on who controls exactly what, when and who performs the work,[225] it soon became clear that such an approach was not always definitive, and alternative tests were developed.[226] The 'Integration Test' sought to consider the extent to which a worker performed their duties as an 'integral' part of the business or as an 'accessory' to the business[227] while the 'Entrepreneurial Test' assessed whether a worker could make a profit or a loss depending on how efficiently they performed the work.[228] The 'Self-Description Test' was also applied in various cases.[229] In more recent times, an increasing focus has been placed on the so-called Mixed Test or Mutuality of Obligations Test, whereby regard is had to the totality of the working relationship with all the elements of the various tests taken into consideration.[230]

222. *See*, generally, Ailbhe Murphy & Maeve Regan, *Employment Law* (2nd ed., Bloomsbury, 2017).
223. Discrimination cannot arise in employment in relation to recruitment, promotion, pay, working conditions, training or experience and dismissal, *see* s. 8 of the Employment Equality Act 1998 (as amended). Discrimination is defined in the legislation as treating one person in a less favourable way than another person based on any one of nine grounds, *see* s. 6.
224. *See* the English case of *Market Investigations Ltd v. Minister for Social Security* [1969] 2 QB 173.
225. *Roche v. Patrick Kelly & Co. Ltd* [1969] IR 100.
226. *DPP v. McLoughlan* [1986] IR 355.
227. *The Sunday Tribune Ltd (in liquidation)* [1984] IR 505.
228. *McDermot v. Loy* (29 Jul. 1982, Unrep, High Court).
229. *O' Coindealbhain (Inspector of Taxes) v. Mooney* [1990] 1 IR 422; *Denny & Sons Limited v. Minister for Social Welfare* [1998] IR 34.
230. *Denny & Sons Limited v. Minister for Social Welfare* [1998] IR 34; *Castleisland Cattle Breeders Society v. Minister for Social, Community and Family Affairs* [2004] IESC 40; *ESB v. Minister for Social, Community and Family Affairs* [2006] IEHC 59; *Kirwan v. Technical Engineering & Electrical Union* [2005] IEHC 5; *Minister for Agriculture and Food v. Barry & Others* [2009] 1 IR 215; *Murphy v. Grand Circle Travel* [2014] IEHC 337.

Chapter 2. Religious Ministers and Labour Law

§1. Status of Ministers of Religion in Ireland

116. Having regard to the separation of church and state in Ireland, few references exist in Irish legislation to ministers of religion. Akin to the separationist systems in France and the Netherlands, it seems that religious ministers in Ireland are regarded as self-employed and, as a result, do not (generally) enjoy the legal rights that attach to employment.[231] Casey noted almost twenty-five years ago, 'Though clear modern authority on the point is lacking, it seems probable that persons in Holy Orders or under religious vows do not have a contractual relationship with their ecclesiastical superiors.'[232] Little definitive case law has emerged in the interim from the Superior Courts to displace this view.[233]

117. Moreover – and in line with Article 44.2.5°, which ensures the right for every religious denomination to manage its own affairs, own, acquire and administer property, and maintain institutions for religious or charitable purposes – Irish law is observed to be 'significantly more protective of the ethos of religious employers than EC law'.[234] Given the denominational autonomy guaranteed for religious organisations in the State, therefore, it appears they may discriminate as to who they might appoint.[235] It is also worthwhile to note that the clergy are free to determine their own working hours.

---

231. *See Wright v. Day* [1895] 2 IR 337 where the court held that an employment relationship did not exist between a chaplain and the trustees of a chapel (which included two Church of Ireland bishops). More recently, in *Millen v. Presbyterian Church in Ireland* (2000) ELR 292, the Employment Appeals Tribunal found that the relationship of employer/employee did not exist as between a Presbyterian Minister and the Presbyterian Church, notwithstanding that the terminology was used in a P60 issued to the plaintiff. *See also Representative Church Body v. Frazer* (2005) ELR 292.
232. James Casey, 'State and Church in Ireland' in Gerhard Robbers (ed.) *State and Church in the European Union* 147, 161 (Nomos Verlagsgesellshaft, 1996). Similarly, Barry Forde, 'Church of Ireland Clergy and Employment Law' 178 *Law & Justice – The Christian Law Review* 80, 85 (2017) notes that given 'the clearer separation between church and state, and allied to protections offered to religious organisations, there may be less scope to infer that clergy might be understood as employees or workers under Irish legislation'. *See also* Norman Doe, *Law and Religion in Europe: A Comparative Introduction* 128–129 (OUP, 2011).
233. However, as Anthony Kerr, 'The Concept of Employee: The Position in Ireland' in Bernd Waas & Guus Heerma van Voss (eds) *Restatement of Labour Law in Europe Vol I: The Concept of Employee* notes at endnote 24 (2017), 'A priest may have, independently of his relationship with his church, a contract of employment with a third party.' In this regard, he notes the case of *Irish Prison Service v. Morris* (FTD 3/2007). *See also* Anthony Kerr, 'Church and Labour Law in Ireland' in *Churches and Labour Law in EC Countries* 329 (European Consortium for Church and State Research, 1993).
234. Gerry Whyte, 'Protecting Religious Ethos in Employment Law: A Clash of Cultures' 27 *Dublin University Law Journal* 169 (2005).
235. *See* Mark Coen, 'Religious Ethos and Employment Equality: A Comparative Irish Perspective' 28(3) *Legal Studies* 452 (2008) and above Part IV, Ch. 1 for the concerns raised in this regard by the UN Human Rights Committee. Having regard to controversies in relation to schools admissions policies (considered further in Part IX), Eoin Daly, *Religion, Law and the Irish State* 165 (Clarus, 2012) suggests it is more 'plausible' that teachers are integral to the ethos of a school than any need for a majority of denominational pupils. *See also* Part VII Ch. 7.

§2. Ministers of Religion and Social Protection

118. Notwithstanding the general lack of consideration afforded to the employment status of ministers of religion in Ireland, one issue which has attracted some attention is in relation to social insurance. Despite being initially excluded, the Social Welfare Act 1974 provided that ministers of religion who engaged exclusively with pastoral works for which they were remunerated could be admitted to social insurance on the application of the appropriate representative body or authority. Inclusion in the social insurance scheme was thus subject to an application being submitted by an appropriate authority or body acting on behalf of the relevant ministers to the Minister for Social Welfare that the services they performed and conditions of their appointment were equivalent to other occupations which were already covered for social insurance purposes. Inclusion was then subject to the agreement of the Minister for Social Welfare. Although access was opened to all religious authorities or bodies, only the Church of Ireland availed of this provision. As a result, ministers of religion employed by the Church of Ireland Representative Body pay Class E Pay Related Social Insurance (PRSI) covering all social insurance payments except Jobseeker's Benefit and Occupational Injuries Benefit.[236]

119. Cognisant that a large number of clergy and religious groups other than the Church of Ireland Representative Body continued to remain without social insurance coverage, the Commission on Social Welfare considered the issue and presented certain recommendations in its 1986 Report.[237] Building on the proposals advanced, reforms were introduced which saw religious who were mainly employed in schools, hospitals and other institutions and undertaking 'what might be termed secular employment as employees under a contract of service'[238] come within the social protection system as employees, insurable at the ordinary or modified rate, as appropriate to their particular circumstances. As a result, ministers of religion who are employed in the public or private sector now benefit from the same level of coverage as other employees in those sectors and are generally insurable under Class A or Class D PRSI.

120. Nonetheless, ministers of religion involved in pastoral care only remained outside the scope of social protection. The Social Welfare (Insurance Inclusions and Exclusions) Regulations 1988 subsequently made it obligatory for the self-employed, including ministers of religions, to pay Class S PRSI in circumstances where they met the minimum income threshold.[239] Consequently, a large proportion of members of the clergy or other ministers of religions were caught and are now

---

236. For more on social security law in Ireland, generally, *see* Mel Cousins & Gerry Whyte, *Social Security Law Ireland* (Wolters Kluwer, 4th ed. 2021).

237. Department of Social Welfare, *Report of the Commission on Social Welfare* (The Stationary Office, 1986).

238. *Dáil Éireann* Debate, Tuesday – 16 Jan. 2018 available at, https://www.oireachtas.ie/en/debates/question/2018-01-16/1661/ (accessed 27 Aug. 2019).

239. From a taxation perspective, remunerated ministers of religion in Ireland are considered to be self-employed under the Taxes Consolidation Act 1997 (as amended). Some religious organisations have sought to support its clergy by providing information documents on the issue, *see*, for

eligible for contributory state pensions. Despite this, questions continue to be raised as to the viability of backdating to 1973 social insurance coverage for members of religious orders who were excluded prior to the introduction of the 1988 Regulations.[240] In response to queries as to the estimated cost of such a move, in 2018, the then Minister for Employment Affairs and Social Protection, Regina Doherty, stated such reform was not on the political agenda:

> It is not possible to cost the backdating of social insurance to the members of religious orders because of various unknown factors, for example, the various contingencies that could have arisen for those members in the intervening period, the question of whether any such backdating should be at the higher or lower rates of payment and the recoupment of contributions for the period in question … there are no plans to backdate social insurance benefits to those who were excluded from social insurance in the past.[241]

121. Unlike in England and Wales, there has been little discussion in either academic or public discourse in Ireland as to the appropriateness of the classification of ministers of religions as self-employed.[242] Yet, given the context outlined above, some religious are increasingly campaigning to be recognised as employees with particular focus being placed on the apparent discrimination many feel they continue to suffer in relation to social insurance and pensions.[243] Central to these grievances is that although employees and those that are self-employed pay the same individual rate of PRSI (currently 4% of gross income), employees also benefit from additional employer contributions, which can rise to 10.85%. Workers classed as self-employed (such as ministers for religion engaged exclusively with pastoral care) do not benefit from employer PRSI contributions which directly affect, in particular, pension entitlements.[244] Whether these informal and seemingly ad hoc campaigns will result in any reforming measures being introduced at a legislative level, however, seems unlikely.

---

example, https://www.ireland.anglican.org/cmsfiles/pdf/Resources/ClergyInfo/2017/ClergyTaxPanel-RoI.pdf (accessed 27 Aug. 2019).

240. *Dáil Éireann* Debate, Tuesday – 16 Jan. 2018 available at https://www.oireachtas.ie/en/debates/question/2018-01-16/1661/ (accessed 27 Aug. 2019). A question as to the feasibility of such reform was raised by Deputy Robert Troy.

241. *Dáil Éireann* Debate, Tuesday – 16 Jan. 2018 available at https://www.oireachtas.ie/en/debates/question/2018-01-16/1661/ (accessed 27 Aug. 2019).

242. For academic commentary, *see* Barry Forde, 'Church of Ireland Clergy and Employment Law' 178 *Law & Justice – The Christian Law Review* 80 (2017).

243. *See* Fr Mattie Long, 'The Retirement of Priests' (Association of Catholic Priests, 2018) available at https://associationofcatholicpriests.ie/the-retirement-of-priests/ (accessed 9 Jun. 2023).

244. *See* https://www.citizensinformation.ie/en/social-welfare/irish-social-welfare-system/social-insurance-prsi/social-insurance-classes/ (accessed 29 Feb. 2024). While Church of Ireland ministers belong to approved pension schemes and have a fixed retirement income which they can rely on, it appears Roman Catholic priests do not thus exacerbating the apparent vulnerability. *See* Cian Molloy, 'Care and Consistency Needed Around the Retirement of Priests' (2018) available at https://www.catholicireland.net/acp-conference-hears-priestly-pension-problems-aplenty/ (accessed 9 Jun. 2023).

§3. Minister of Religion Permission

122. One area of recent Irish legislative engagement which specifically addresses employment in the context of religious communities is that relating to permission to work as a minister of religion in the jurisdiction. A new preclearance procedure was introduced in April 2018 (revised in November 2022) and applies to both visa and non-visa-required non-EEA (European Economic Area) nationals. Pursuant to the Minister of Religion Permission, qualifying religious personnel will be permitted to enter and remain in the Irish State for up to three years, 'where there is a demonstrated need for their services and subject to compliance with all other immigration requirements that apply in individual cases'.[245] Where a non-EEA national (both visa required and non-visa required) has been offered a job with a religious body or faith community as a minister of religion in Ireland, he/she must seek prior approval to work in that capacity from the Irish Immigration Service of the Department of Justice, before travelling to the State.

123. In order to obtain permission to work as a minister of religion, the work of the minister must include all or most of the following for 'a religious or faith community already established in the State':

- conducting spiritual worship and or ceremonies to an established congregation in Ireland;
- giving pastoral care to members of an established congregation or faith community through preaching;
- conducting classes based on a religious ethos, supervising prayer meetings, etc.;
- providing spiritual leadership to an established faith community in Ireland; an established church is defined as a church supported by the government as a national institution;
- ministering to the spiritual needs of a congregation;
- pastoral visitation;
- providing senior administration support of a substantially full-time nature to a religious institution/ order/ church where the work would not qualify for an employment permit issued by the Department of Business, Enterprise and Innovation;
- being a member of a religious community that takes public vows of poverty, chastity and obedience.[246]

124. Applicants who successfully secure such permission are prohibited from working as volunteers or engaging in study unless such activity does not interfere

245. *See* https://www.irishimmigration.ie/wp-content/uploads/2022/12/Minister-of-Religion-Policy-Document.pdf (accessed 9 Jun. 2023). *See also* https://www.irishimmigration.ie/coming-to-work-in-ireland/what-are-my-options-for-working-in-ireland/coming-to-work-for-more-than-90-days/minister-of-religion/#scheme.

246. *See* https://www.irishimmigration.ie/wp-content/uploads/2021/04/Minister-of-Religion-permission.pdf (accessed 9 Jun. 2023). Note, difficulties with the definition and criteria applied have been highlighted by, in particular, the Association of Missionaries and Religious of Ireland, *see* Colin Coyle, 'Church complains that visa problems are hitting ministry in Ireland' *The Times*, 15 Mar. 2020.

with their primary role as minister. Furthermore, although a successful applicant may be accompanied by his/her family (spouses/partners and children under 18 or in full-time education or otherwise dependent subject to a maximum age of 23), his/her permission to remain is dependent on the residence status of the minister of religion within Ireland and extends only for the period of his/her permission.

125. Although the new preclearance procedure is ostensibly 'to facilitate and streamline entry to the State of Ministers of Religion from non-EEA states',[247] it has been suggested such reforms reflect a Government policy aimed at restricting the number of immigrants moving to Ireland to work as religious ministers or volunteers.[248]

247. *See* http://www.inis.gov.ie/en/INIS/Pages/minister-of-religion-permission (accessed 27 Aug. 2019).
248. 'Religious Ministers Subject to New Irish Visa Rules' (*Metro Éireann*, 15 May 2018) *see* http://www.metroeireann.com/news/1303/religious-ministers-subject-to-new-irish-visa-rules.html (accessed 1 Mar. 2021).

Chapter 3. Other Church Employees and Labour Law

126. Although church volunteers will not be regarded as employees under Irish employment law, many lay workers may be under a contract of employment with church bodies. Where such a contract exists, secretaries, cleaners, musicians or other laypersons employed by a diocese, convent or other religious body will be held in the same position as any other employee and enjoy all attendant employment-related rights under Irish law.[249] In an Irish context, it is also important to note that the Boards of Management of public, religious-run schools are employers, for example, of teachers, notwithstanding that they are paid by the State.[250]

249. *See*, for example, *Parish Secretary v. Parish Office* (26/4/2018) (ADJ-00012539, Workplace Relations Commission).

250. *See* Part IX for more on the role of Boards of Management. Note, in *O'Keeffe v. Hickey* [2008] IESC 72, a majority of the Supreme Court held that the Minister for Education and the State could not be held vicariously liable for sexual assaults by a National School principal on an eight-year-old girl because there was no formal or substantive employer/employee relationship between them. *See also*, however, *O'Keeffe v. Ireland*, Application No. 35810/09, 28 Jan. 2014 (Grand Chamber, European Court of Human Rights).

Part VII. Religious Communities and Protections of the Individual

Introduction

127. In this part, we will examine various ways in which particular laws impact both religious groups and individuals. In addition to addressing well-established legal principles or legislation, specific attention will also be afforded to new developments in the various areas of law. In relation to privacy, Chapter 1 will consider both the constitutionally recognised right to privacy and the impact of the EU GDPR. Chapter 2 will turn to consider the freedom to marry under Irish law placing a special focus on the introduction of the remedy divorce (and the right to remarry) in the jurisdiction and recent developments in relation to same-sex marriage. It will then consider the degrees of relationship where marriage is still prohibited under Irish law. Drawing attention to Article 40.6.1° of the Irish Constitution, Chapter 3 considers the freedom of expression in Ireland and the recent developments in relation to blasphemy before Chapter 4 investigates the position of religious tribunals in Ireland and Irish law on oath-taking. Chapter 5 focuses on the role of sacerdotal privilege in Irish law, while Chapter 6 addresses issues of medical ethics, in particular, conscientious objection clauses. Chapter 7 looks at Irish equality legislation, while Chapter 8 closes the part by considering how penal law and religion interact in modern Ireland, placing the spotlight on religious worship and hate crime, in particular.

Chapter 1. Protection of Privacy

128. Article 40.3 of the Irish Constitution states: 'The State guarantees in its laws to respect, and as far as practicable, by its laws to defend and vindicate the personal rights of the citizen.'[251] Although there is no express constitutional provision relating to privacy, the right to privacy has been recognised as an unenumerated right flowing from Article 40.3. As a result, the Working Group on Privacy within the Department of Justice and Equality observed in 2006:

> It follows that the law in Ireland by virtue of these constitutional protections, affords clear and established remedies against the State for intrusions on privacy interests. Legislation which interferes with those interests and which either does so other than for the purposes of securing a clear objective in the common good, or which seeks to secure such an objective in a manner that is not proportionate to the right of privacy infringed, is liable to invalidation. The activities of State agents who interfere with such privacy entitlements without due and lawful authority or justification may similarly present an actionable violation. A person who apprehends an interference with his or her privacy rights by the State may seek injunctive relief to prevent such interference, and a person who suffers damage as a consequence of such an interference, may seek to recover damages against the State.[252]

129. While the full scope of the constitutional protection remains unclear, it has been noted that it is 'probable that the dimensions of the right as it develops before the Irish Courts will be influenced by the approach of the European Court of Human Rights'.[253] Article 8 of the ECHR seeks to enshrine the right to respect for personal and family life. It states:

a. Everyone has the right to respect for his private and family life, his home and his correspondence.
b. There shall be no interference by a public authority with the exercise of this right except such as is in accordance with the law and is necessary in a democratic society in the interests of national security, public safety or the economic well-being of the country, for the prevention of disorder or crime, for the protection of health or morals, or for the protection of the rights and freedoms of others.'

---

251. A right to marital privacy was recognised in *McGee v. The Attorney General* [1973] IR 284 where Walsh J in the Supreme Court held that 'Article 41 of the Constitution guarantees the husband and wife against … invasion of their privacy by the State.' A general right to privacy was subsequently recognised in *Kennedy and Arnold v. Ireland* [1987] IR 587 having been strongly hinted at in *Norris v. Attorney General* [1984] IR 36. *See also Haughey v. Moriarty* [1999] 3 IR 1, 58.
252. *Report of Working Group on Privacy* (2006) 34 available at, http://www.justice.ie/en/JELR/WkgGrpPrivacy.pdf/Files/WkgGrpPrivacy.pdf (accessed 28 Aug. 2019).
253. *Report of Working Group on Privacy* (2006) 33 available at http://www.justice.ie/en/JELR/WkgGrpPrivacy.pdf/Files/WkgGrpPrivacy.pdf (accessed 28 Aug. 2019). *See also* Hilary Delany & Eoin Carolan, *The Right to Privacy: A Doctrinal and Comparative Analysis* (Thomson Roundhall, 2008); Eoin Carolan & Ailbhe O'Neill, *Media Law in Ireland* 367–470 (2nd ed., Bloomsbury Professional, 2019).

130. As noted in Part IV Chapter 2, the ECHR, although ratified by Ireland in 1953, only became part of Ireland's domestic law through the enactment of the ECHR Act 2003. Section 2(1) of the 2003 Act provides:

> in interpreting and applying any statutory provision or rule of law, a court shall, in so far as is possible, subject to the rules of law relating to such interpretation and application, do so in a manner compatible with the State's obligations under the Convention provisions.

131. Consequently, a right to privacy now exists in Irish law both under the Irish Constitution and under the ECHR. The right to respect for private and family life is also guaranteed by Article 17 of the ICCPR. The ability of states to interfere with peoples' privacy is thus limited to circumstances when it is deemed necessary and proportionate to achieving a legitimate aim.

132. Even more specific privacy rights may be found in Irish data protection legislation and under key EU regulations.[254] The recent EU GDPR represents a particularly significant intervention in this regard. Aiming to ensure a more uniform interpretation and application of data protection standards across the EU, the GDPR has increased the standards of data protection for individuals and heightened the obligations of organisations that process personal data.[255]

133. As an EU regulation, the GDPR has direct effect under Irish law. However, certain legislative interventions have been required. Updating the previous data protection framework applied under the Data Protection Acts 1988 and 2003, the Data Protection Act 2018 has now established a new Data Protection Commission acting as the State's data protection authority.[256] Furthermore, the 2018 Act transposed an accompanying EU Law Enforcement Directive into domestic law, which seeks to establish data protection standards in relation to criminal offences and penalties, increasing the range of possible sanctions for infringements of the new rules. The 2018 Act also addressed those areas of the GDPR where flexibility is afforded to the Member States,[257] thereby giving fuller effect to GDPR provisions.

134. In terms of the impact of these developments on religious law, two main effects may be noted. First, among the special categories of personal data deemed 'sensitive' and receiving specific protection under the GDPR is that concerning religious or philosophical beliefs. Pursuant to Article 9(1), processing of such data is prohibited, albeit certain derogations are carried in subsection (2).[258]

135. Second, where religious bodies or organisations store data, they will be required to comply with the new framework. For example, pursuant to Article 37 of

---

254. Note, there is no general right to privacy at a legislative level.
255. For more information on GDPR, *see*, https://ec.europa.eu/info/law/law-topic/data-protection_en.
256. https://www.dataprotection.ie/ (accessed 7 Sep. 2023).
257. For example, regarding the digital age of consent.
258. A company or organisation may be allowed to process sensitive personal data if, for example, a data subject has provided explicit consent.

the GDPR, private undertakings (including religious organisations) are required to appoint a Data Protection Officer if their core activity consists of regular and systematic monitoring of data subjects on a large scale or if their activities consist of large-scale processing of special categories of sensitive data including, for example, data on religious and political beliefs.[259] Various religious organisations in Ireland have now set out detailed privacy statements online. The Archdiocese of Dublin notes that the Archbishop is 'the sole controller of the personal data and special category data contained in the Baptism Registers held in Parishes of the Archdiocese with respect to storage and retention of data, standard and special annotation of data and alteration of data' while the Archbishop, along with the Parish Priest/Administrator/Moderator assigned to the Parish which holds the Baptism Register, 'are each a joint controller of the personal data and special category data with respect to collecting and recording of data' in the Register.[260] This statement also explains how the Archdiocese processes information, including personal data, that it receives.[261]

259. Public sector bodies, other than courts acting in their judicial capacity, are required to appoint a Data Protection Officer, irrespective of their processing activities.
260. *See*, https://www.dublindiocese.ie/privacy-policy/ (accessed 7 Sep. 2023).
261. *See*, https://www.dublindiocese.ie/privacy-policy/ (accessed 7 Sep. 2023).

Chapter 2. Freedom to Marry

§1. Introduction

136. As Nussbaum notes: 'For many if not most people … marriage is not a trivial matter. It is a key to the pursuit of happiness, something people aspire to – and keep on aspiring to, again and again, even when their experience has been far from happy.'[262] The importance of marriage in an Irish context remains constant, with the right to marry long regarded as an unenumerated right under Article 40.3 of the Irish Constitution.[263] Notwithstanding the growth in cohabitation rates over recent decades[264] and the introduction of cohabitation legislation,[265] cohabitation remains seen 'as a step in progression towards marriage'.[266] As a result, Connolly notes, 'The predominance of marriage as a basis for family formation is … essentially intact.'[267] Reflecting on this importance, the freedom to marry has been extended under Irish law in recent decades with same-sex marriage available in the jurisdiction since 2015.[268]

§2. Divorce: Freedom to Remarry

137. As originally enacted in 1937, Article 41.3.2° of the Irish Constitution introduced a ban on divorce, providing: 'No law shall be enacted providing for the grant of a dissolution of marriage.'[269] From the early 1970s, however, marital breakdown and the need for divorce were drawing increasing public attention. A 1995 referendum ultimately resulted in the amendment of Article 41.3.2° of the Constitution

262. Marta Nussbaum, 'A Right to Marry?' 98(3) *California Law Review* 667, 668 (2010).
263. *See*, for example, *O'Shea and O'Shea v. Ireland & the Attorney General* [2007] 1 ILRM 460; *Ryan v. Attorney General* [1965] IR 294.
264. *See* Linda Connolly, 'Locating the Irish Family' in Linda Connolly (ed.) *The 'Irish' Family* (Routledge, 2015).
265. *See* the Civil Partnership and Certain Rights and Obligations of Cohabitants Act 2010 discussed further at Part X Ch. 1.
266. Margaret Fine-Davis, *Attitudes to Family Formation in Ireland: Findings from the Nationwide Study* (Family Support Agency, 2011).
267. Linda Connolly, 'Locating the Irish Family' in Linda Connolly (ed.) *The 'Irish' Family* 20 (Routledge, 2015).
268. Reflecting on the judicial, legislative and constitutional developments that culminated in the passing of the marriage equality referendum in 2015, Fergus Ryan, '21st Century Families: 19th Century Values; Modern Family Law in the Shadow of the Constitution' in Eoin Carolan and Oran Doyle (eds), The Irish Constitution: Governance and Values (Thomson Round Hall, 2008) 64 notes: 'The fervour of the struggle for same-sex marriage underpinned the importance of marriage as an institution … This exaltation of marriage … necessarily implies that other family arrangements are "lesser than" and not as significant as families based on marriage … '. He adds: 'The constitutional privilege for the marital family remains, and may well even have been compounded by the referendum outcome.' For more on the legal and constitutional importance of marriage and marital status, *see* Ch. X.
269. Although in keeping with the religio-cultural norms of the majority in 1937, it is interesting to note that the more secular First Constitution of the Irish Free State in 1922 did not carry such a ban. Note, foreign divorces could be recognised notwithstanding this ban.

to provide for divorce and enumerating the basic criteria to be fulfilled to successfully obtain such a decree.[270] The Family Law (Divorce) Act 1996 subsequently came into effect on 27 February 1997, supplementing the new constitutional provision and empowering the judiciary to order a decree of divorce and financial relief (ancillary provision).[271] Former (and now divorced) spouses were, for the first time since 1937, afforded the freedom to legally remarry in Ireland following marital breakdown.

§3. Same-Sex Marriage under Irish Law

138. While the introduction of divorce ensured the freedom to marry was extended to a cohort of the public formerly denied the right, other segments of society remained unable to access the institution. In particular, acting as a barrier to same-sex couples, marriage continued to be viewed under Irish law as the voluntary union of 'one man and one woman to the exclusion of all others'.[272] Although the Civil Partnership and Certain Rights and Obligations of Cohabitants Act 2010 saw the introduction of same-sex civil partnership into Irish law, advocacy groups campaigning for marriage equality were gaining ever-increasing traction throughout the first decades of the twenty-first century. A referendum on the Thirty-Fourth Amendment of the Constitution – the so-called Marriage Equality Referendum – was held in 2015 and passed by 62% with a 60% turnout.[273] Ireland thus became the first country to introduce marriage equality by popular vote.[274] Article 41.4 now provides that 'marriage may be contracted in accordance with law by two parties without distinction as to their sex'. At a legislative level, same-sex marriage is also facilitated through the Marriage Act 2015, while entry into same-sex civil partnership closed in 2015.

270. *See* Part X for more on the criteria for divorce.
271. For a more on the historical development of divorce in Ireland and the difficulties identified with the Irish regime, *see* Kathryn O'Sullivan, 'The Legacy Continues: Ancillary Relief on Divorce in Ireland' 25(3) *Journal of Family Studies* 337 (2019).
272. *TF v. Ireland* [1995] IR 321 per Costello J. This description seemed in line with the traditional definition advanced by Lord Penzance in *Hyde v. Hyde* [1866] LR 1 P & D 130: 'I conceive that marriage, as understood in Christendom, may for this purpose be defined as the voluntary union for life of one man and one woman, to the exclusion of all others.'
273. Note, Brian Tobin, *The Legal Recognition of Same-Sex Relationships: Emerging Families in Ireland and Beyond* (Hart Publishing, 2023) Ch. 1 is critical of the Government's decision to hold such a referendum, arguing that marriage equality could and should have been effected through legislative reform.
274. *See* Éanna O'Caollaí & Mark Hillard, 'Ireland Becomes First Country to Approve Same-Sex Marriage by Popular Vote' *Irish Times*, 23 May 2015. The referendum was recommended by the Constitutional Convention. For more on the introduction of same-sex marriage, *see* Brian Tobin, *The Legal Recognition of Same-Sex Relationships: Emerging Families in Ireland and Beyond* (Hart Publishing, 2023) Ch. 1; Susan Leahy & Kathryn O'Sullivan, 'Changing Conceptions of Marriage in Ireland: Law and Practice' 30(3) *Child and Family Law Quarterly* 279 (2018).

§4. Prohibited Degrees of Relationships

139. Despite these developments in widening access to marriage, marital relationships between certain categories of persons remain forbidden in Ireland: the prohibited degrees of relationship are still those originally regarded as void for the purposes of the Marriage Act 1835 (as amended). This, it is understood, ensures that marriages caught by the earlier Marriages Act 1537 continue to be viewed as void ab initio under Irish law.[275]

140. On the basis of 'consanguinity', the prohibition on marriage extends as far as blood relationships in the third degree.[276] As a result, a woman is prohibited from marrying her grandfather, father, uncle, brother, son, grandson or nephew, and a man is prohibited from marrying his grandmother, mother, aunt, sister, daughter, granddaughter or niece.[277] Moreover, on the basis of 'affinity', a woman is forbidden from marrying the former husband of her grandmother, mother, aunt, daughter, niece or granddaughter.[278] She is similarly prohibited from marrying her former husband's grandfather, father, uncle, son, nephew or grandson. Equivalent prohibitions also apply to men.

141. As initially enacted, a person was prohibited from marrying the brother or sister of a former spouse. This was removed with the introduction of the Deceased Wife's Sister's Marriage Act 1907 as amended by the Deceased Brother's Widow's Marriage Act 1921. These enactments only permitted such marriages, however, where the first spouse was deceased. As a result of the 2006 Irish High Court (IEHC) decision of *O'Shea and O'Shea v. Ireland & the Attorney General*,[279] it is now also permissible to marry a former spouse's sibling where the first marriage was terminated by divorce.

142. The impediments to marriage based on consanguinity and affinity outlined above have recently been extended, 'subject to any necessary modifications', to same-sex marriages. Section 5 of the Marriage Act 2015 inserts a new section 2A into the Civil Registration Act 2004, which provides:

> (1) For the purposes of this Act, any prohibition in this Act or any other enactment or rule of law on marriage between two persons of the opposite sex arising by virtue of a relationship of consanguinity or affinity between

275. However, note the potential impact of the newly discovered Marriage Act (No. 2) 1537, *see* Meabh Harding, 'The Curious Incident of the Marriage Act (No 2) 1537 and the Irish Statute Book' 32(1) *Legal Studies* 78 (2012).
276. Note, these prohibitions apply equally to relationships of the half-blood as to the whole blood, however, they do not apply to relationships by adoption.
277. As John Mee, 'Marriage Partnership and the Prohibited Degrees of Relationship' 27 *Irish Law Times* 259 (2009) highlights, however, a marriage with one's great-grandparent, a relation in the third degree, is permitted.
278. *See* Henry A. Finlay, 'Farewell to Affinity and the Calculus of Kinship' 5(1) *University of Tasmania Law Review* 16, 19 (1975) for a consideration of prohibitions on the basis of affinity generally.
279. [2007] 1 ILRM 460.

them, shall, subject to any necessary modifications, apply to marriage between two persons of the same sex as it applies to marriage between two persons of the opposite sex.

(2) A marriage purported to be solemnised which contravenes a prohibition referred to in subsection (1) shall be void.[280]

280. For a critique of the prohibitions to marriage under Irish law, *see* Kathryn O'Sullivan, 'Access to Marriage: Consanguinity and Affinity Prohibitions in National and International Context' 22(2) *Irish Journal of Family Law* 8 (2019).

Chapter 3. Freedom of Expression

§1. Introduction

143. Article 40.6.1° of the Irish Constitution provides that the State guarantees liberty for the rights of the citizens to freely express their convictions and opinions. The exercise of these rights is not absolute, however, but rather 'subject to public order and morality'. Pursuant to Article 40.6.1°:

> The State guarantees liberty for the exercise of the following rights, subject to public order and morality: –
>
> i The right of the citizens to express freely their convictions and opinions.
> The education of public opinion being, however, a matter of such grave import to the common good, the State shall endeavour to ensure that organs of public opinion, such as the radio, the press, the cinema, while preserving their rightful liberty of expression, including criticism of Government policy, shall not be used to undermine public order or morality or the authority of the State ….

144. Particular issues have arisen in Ireland in relation to associated provisions concerning blasphemy.

§2. Blasphemy under Irish Law

145. In addition to the foregoing provisions, Article 40.6.1°.i of the Irish Constitution included a further provision which, as originally enacted, stated: 'The publication or utterance of blasphemous, seditious, or indecent matter is an offence which shall be punishable in accordance with law.'[281] Thus, among others, the publication of blasphemous material gave rise to a specific criminal offence.[282] Notwithstanding the constitutional intention, however, in the absence of any statutory definition, the offence remained largely impossible to prosecute for decades.[283] It was only with the introduction of section 36 of the Defamation Act 2009 that the

281. For an early consideration of blasphemy in Ireland, *see* Paul O'Higgins, 'Blasphemy in Irish Law' 23 *Modern Law Review* 151 (1960).

282. *See* Neville Cox, 'The Ethical Case for a Blasphemy Law' in Robert S. Fortner & P. Mark Fackler (eds) *The Handbook of Global Communication and Media Ethics* 263–297 (Wiley-Blackwell, 2011).

283. In *Corway v. Independent Newspapers* [1999] 4 IR 484, Barrington J delivering the judgment of the IESC doubted whether the historical common law offence of blasphemy (as outlined in the House of Lords decision of *Whitehouse v. Lemon* [1979] 1 ALL ER 898) could have survived post-independence in Ireland in the context of the provisions of the Constitution of the Irish Free State in 1922 and latterly of the Second Constitution of Ireland in 1937. As a result, he upheld the High Court's decision and refused the appeal in question to grant the applicant leave to initiate a criminal prosecution for blasphemy under s. 8 of the then Defamation Act 1961. The Court reiterated that it was for the legislature to define the offence of blasphemy.

offence of publishing blasphemous material became enforceable. Section 36(1) stated that a person who published or uttered blasphemous matter was guilty of an offence and was liable upon conviction on indictment to a fine of up to EUR 25,000. Pursuant to section 36(2) of the 2009 Act, a person published or uttered blasphemous matter if:

(a) he or she published or uttered matter that were grossly abusive or insulting in relation to matters held sacred by any religion, thereby causing outrage among a substantial number of the adherents of that religion; and
(b) he or she intended, by the publication or utterance of the matter concerned, to cause such outrage.

146. Given this definition, it appeared that the aim of the legislation was protecting individuals from offence, with the legislative provisions also seeming to place emphasis on the intention of the accused to provoke outrage. Consequently, it has been suggested that 'the modernised rationale' of the Irish statutory offence was 'not to protect the sanctity of religious doctrine as such, but rather to protect religious adherent from gratuitous and offensive forms of abuse, whether written or verbal'.[284] Section 36(3), however, added that it was a defence to proceedings for the defendant to prove that a reasonable person would have found genuine literary, artistic, political, scientific, or academic value in the matter to which the offence related, thus appearing to envisage an objective test.[285]

147. While the introduction of the 2009 legislation made possible the enforcement of the constitutionally referenced offence – and presumably contributed to ensuring that controversial materials such as the Charlie Hebdo cartoons of the Prophet Mohammed were not reproduced in Ireland in 2015[286] – this development came in the face of long-standing calls for the abolition of the reference to blasphemy in Article 40.6.1. In 1991, the Law Reform Commission of Ireland published its Report on the Crime of Libel and called for the reform of the law concerning blasphemy.[287] In 1996, the Constitutional Review Group again called for such abolition regarding the constitutional offence as a potentially illegitimate restriction on the right to freedom of expression.[288] The call was further repeated in 2003 in the Report of the Legal Advisory Group on Defamation established by the

284. Eoin Daly, *Religion, Law and the Irish State* 444 (Clarus, 2012). He also notes at 431 the 'elusive and arguably unworkable definition of blasphemy adopted'.
285. Note, reflecting provisions of the Charities Act 2009 discussed in Part III Ch. 1, s. 36(4) of the Defamation Act 2009 noted that for the purposes of the section, 'religion' did not include an organisation or cult (a) the principal object of which is the making of profit, or (b) that employs oppressive psychological manipulation (i) of its followers, or (ii) for the purpose of gaining new followers.
286. James Car, 'Ireland' in Oliver Scharbrodt et al. (eds) *Yearbook of Muslims in Europe* 363 (Brill, 2015) notes that Ali Selim from the Islamic Cultural Centre of Ireland stated publicly that he would obtain legal advice if the controversial cartoons were reproduced in the jurisdiction. Note, there has, however, been no prosecution for blasphemy in the history of the State.
287. Law Reform Commission, *Report on the Crime of Libel* 12, para. 21 (1991-LRC 41).
288. *Report of the Constitution Review Group* 274 (The Stationery Office, 1996).

Minister for Justice, Equality and Law Reform[289] and in 2008 by an Irish All-Party Joint Oireachtas Committee on the Constitution.[290] Internationally, the UN Human Rights Committee also highlighted its concerns regarding the provisions and added to the calls for reform.[291]

148. Responding to these criticisms – and in the wake of public controversy surrounding the potentially blasphemous statements of comedian Stephen Fry on Raidió Teilifís Éireann's (RTÉ's) The Meaning of Life in 2017[292] – a referendum on the Thirty-Seventh Amendment of the Constitution was held in October 2018 proposing to remove the reference to blasphemy from the Constitution. The referendum was passed by a majority of 65%.[293] In December 2019, the Blasphemy (Abolition of Offences and Related Matters) Act 2019 was signed into law. As well as abolishing 'any rule of law by virtue of which a) blasphemy or b) blasphemous libel, is an offence',[294] it specifically repealed sections 36 and 37 of the Defamation Act 2009.[295]

---

289. *Report of the Legal Advisory Group on Defamation* 121 (The Stationery Office, 2003).
290. Joint Oireachtas Committee on the Constitution, *Article 40.6.1°i: Freedom of Expression* (The Stationery Office, 2008).
291. Human Rights Committee, *Concluding Observations on the Fourth Periodic Report of Ireland* (2014, CCPR/C/IRL/CO/4) available to download at https://tbinternet.ohchr.org/_layouts/15/treatybodyexternal/Download.aspx?symbolno=CCPR/C/IRL/CO/4&Lang=En (accessed 27 Aug. 2019). *See also* Part IV Ch. 1 above.
292. 'Fry could face €25,000 fine over blasphemy complaint' (RTÉ News, 6 May 2017) available at https://www.rte.ie/entertainment/2017/0506/873060-stephen-fry/ (accessed 28 Aug. 2019). No prosecution resulted from the affair. *See also* Eoin Carolan & Ailbhe O'Neill, *Media Law in Ireland* 68 (2nd ed., Bloomsbury Professional, 2019).
293. Article 40.6.1°.i of the Irish Constitution now states: 'The publication or utterance of seditious or indecent matter is an offence which shall be punishable in accordance with law.'
294. Section 1.
295. Section 4.

Chapter 4. Due Process Norms and Religious Groups

§1. Religious Tribunals and the Right to a Fair Trial

149. While to date, there have been no reports of, for example, Sharia Councils existing in Ireland, marriage tribunals of the Roman Catholic Church (as established by the Irish Episcopal Conference in 1975) do operate in the jurisdiction with reports suggesting that these regional First Instance Tribunals 'have a significant case load'.[296] Despite the apparent popularity of such fora, however, it is reasonably well established that religious courts or tribunals in Ireland do not have jurisdiction in the same manner enjoyed by State courts.[297] It is similarly accepted that '[r]eligious divorces or equivalent proceedings conducted in Ireland do not have legal force'.[298] In short, although Irish courts might be required to interpret or develop, for example, canon law,[299] the State does not recognise religious law as a source of law unless and until it is transposed into domestic legislation.[300] In this context, although they may be operating in the jurisdiction, religious courts or tribunals are regarded as private bodies and are thus not subject to judicial review, even in circumstances where there may be questions to be asked as regards the right to a fair trial.[301]

§2. Oath-Taking

150. As a general rule, Irish law requires that evidence must be given on oath or affirmation.[302] The primary legislation in the area remains the Oaths Act 1888 and the Oaths Act 1909. In terms of the wording itself, section 2 of the 1909 Act provides:

---

296. Máiread Enright, '"Preferring the Stranger?" Towards an Irish Approach to Muslim Divorce Practice' 49(1) *Irish Jurist* 65, 71–72 (2013).
297. *O'Keeffe v. Cardinal Cullen* [1873] 7 ILTR 100 at 107.
298. Máiread Enright, '"Preferring the Stranger?" Towards an Irish Approach to Muslim Divorce Practice' 49(1) *Irish Jurist* 65, 71 (2013). She highlights that 'At various points in Irish history it has been suggested that, rather than introduce divorce, the State should recognise church annulments as dissolving marriage, or as permitting legal remarriage … It is instructive that these suggestions have never been taken up and that separate civil divorce was preferred.'
299. *See*, *MM v. PM* [1986] 1 ILRM 515 where the canon law regarding the consummation of marriage was considered. *See also* John McAreavey, *The Canon Law of Marriage and the Family* (Four Courts Press, 1997).
300. For a consideration of how the 'King's canon law' of nullity, specifically, was introduced into Irish law through legislation, *see* Meabh Harding, 'Religion and Family Law in Ireland: From a Catholic Protection of Marriage to a "Catholic" Approach to Nullity' in Jane Mair & Esin Örücü (eds) *The Place of Religion in Family Law* 161 at 163 (Intersentia, 2011). *See also N (Otherwise K) v. K* [1986] 6 ILRM 75.
301. For a consideration as to whether the Irish legislature could legislate to limit or otherwise regulate the activities of any Sharia Council should one begin to operate in Ireland, *see* Máiread Enright, '"Preferring the Stranger?" Towards an Irish Approach to Muslim Divorce Practice' 49(1) *Irish Jurist* 65, 74–77 (2013).
302. The main exceptions are where the witness or deponent is a child under the age of 14 or a person with an intellectual disability, *see* s. 28 of the Children Act 1997.

> The person taking the oath shall hold the New Testament, or, in the case of a Jew, the Old Testament, in his uplifted hand, and shall say or repeat after the officer administering the oath the words 'I swear by Almighty God that … ', followed by the words of the oath prescribed by law.[303]

151. The 1909 Act adds that for deponents of other faiths, 'the oath shall be administered in any manner which is now lawful'. In this context, the practice developed of inquiring what oath a witness or deponent would regard as binding and swearing him/her accordingly.[304] Moreover, pursuant to section 1 of the 1888 Act, affirmation is available where the deponent objects to being sworn on the basis that either they have no religious belief or that the taking of the oath is contrary to their religious belief.

152. Reflecting on the law governing oath-taking, the Law Reform Commission observed in 1990:

> The number of possible binding forms of oath, then, are as infinitely extensible as the possible permutations of human faith. At first sight, this would appear to reflect an admirable degree of flexibility in the law. On examination, however, there are a number of difficulties in the operation of the scheme in respect of persons having a religious faith.[305]

153. As a result, it concluded that the oath should be abolished for witnesses and jurors and for deponents submitting affidavits in all proceedings, whether civil or criminal.[306] Instead, it recommended that any person who may be required to take an oath in judicial proceedings should be required to make a solemn statutory affirmation to the effect:

> I, A.B., do solemnly, sincerely and truly declare and affirm that the evidence I shall give shall be the truth, the whole truth and nothing but the truth. I am aware that if I knowingly give false evidence I may be prosecuted for perjury.[307]

154. Despite these recommendations, no such reform was forthcoming.

155. In 2016, the issue again garnered significant media attention.[308] President of the High Court, Justice Peter Kelly, was highly critical of procedures adopted by

303. Typically, for a witness providing oral testimony, they will be required to add 'that the evidence I shall give shall be the truth, the whole truth and nothing but the truth'.
304. Law Reform Commission, *Report on Oaths ad Affirmations* 16 (1990-LRC 34).
305. Law Reform Commission, *Report on Oaths ad Affirmations* 18 (1990-LRC 34).
306. Law Reform Commission, *Report on Oaths ad Affirmations* 43 (1990-LRC 34).
307. Law Reform Commission, *Report on Oaths ad Affirmations* 43 (1990-LRC 34).
308. *See*, for example, Mark O'Regan, 'Solicitors Told to Carry Bible and Koran' *Irish Independent*, 24 Apr. 2016.

solicitors with regard to oath-taking, finding in the case before him that as the deponent had not been furnished with a Bible when swearing the oath in question, the swearing of the affidavit involved was invalid.[309] The court was equally critical of suggestions that in the absence of a Bible, the deponent should have affirmed rather than sworn the affidavit.[310] While the right to affirm is recognised in the Oaths Act 1888, it would, according to the court, have been an abuse of the right to rely on it in circumstances where the appropriate religious text was unavailable. Arising from this case, it has been reported that the Law Society of Ireland issued a circular to members advising them of the need to carry a copy of the Bible and the Koran during working hours in order to best ensure the validity of oaths administered.[311] While the 2016 circular was not made public, the Law Society of Ireland subsequently reiterated the need for reform, noting the 'burden' placed on practitioners and their clients by the procedural requirement of religious oaths and 'even the enquiry as to preference of affirmations'.[312]

156. Perhaps influenced by these pressures, the Law Reform Commission again considered the issue in its Report on the Consolidation and Reform of Aspects of the Law of Evidence launched in January 2017.[313] It recommended that the provisions in the Oaths Acts 1888 and 1909 concerning the taking of oaths and affirmations 'should be replaced by provisions in the draft Evidence Bill that a person may give sworn testimony on oath or affirmation without the need when testifying by affirmation to indicate religious belief'.[314] The Commission also recommended that the 1888 and 1909 Acts be repealed in their entirety.

157. Section 21 of the Civil and Criminal Law (Miscellaneous) Act 2020 goes some way towards addressing the shortcomings identified with the introduction of a framework for 'Statements of Truth' into Irish law. Section 21(2) provides:

---

309. *In re Hennessy and Davidson* (4 Apr. 2016, High Court, *ex tempore*). *See* Emile Burke-Murphy, 'Affidavits Must Be Administered on Religious Text' 34 *Irish Law Times* 126 (2016). Note, Kelly J is not the only member of the judiciary to chastise practitioners in this regard. In *SA v. Refugee Appeal Tribunal and others* [2012] IEHC 8 at [10], Hogan J also noted 'a certain laxness and complacency has crept into the practice of swearing of affidavits'.
310. *See* Colette Reid, 'Nothing But the Truth' *Law Society Gazette* 34 (May 2016).
311. Mark O'Regan, 'Solicitors Told to Carry Bible and Koran' *Irish Independent*, 24 Apr. 2016. Note the findings of *Census 2022 Profile 5-Diversity, Migration, Ethnicity, Irish Travellers & Religion* which show the range of religious diversity in Ireland today, *see* https://www.cso.ie/en/releasesandpublications/ep/p-cpp5/census2022profile5-diversitymigrationethnicityirishtravellersreligion/religion/ (accessed 01.Nov.2023).
312. Law Society of Ireland, *Policy and Law Reform Agenda* (December 2017) 2 available at https://www.lawsociety.ie/globalassets/documents/policy-and-law-reform/public-affairs/plr-newsletter-dec2017.pdf (accessed 1 Nov. 2023). Having regard to these difficulties, the Society notes it 'continues to argue for reform to the requirement for religious oaths, in favour of a universal affirmation'.
313. The Law Reform Commission, *Report on the Consolidation and Reform of Aspects of the Law of Evidence* 350–351 (2016-LRC117).
314. The Law Reform Commission, *Report on the Consolidation and Reform of Aspects of the Law of Evidence* 351 (2016-LRC117).

A statement of truth –

(a) may be in electronic form,
(b) shall contain a statement that the person making the statement of truth has an honest belief that the facts stated therein are true,
(c) may be signed by the person making it by that person entering his or her name in an electronic format or otherwise electronically as may be permitted by rules of court, and
(d) shall comply with any other requirements as to its content, verification, authentication or form as may be prescribed by rules of court.[315]

158. However, as per section 21(1), such statements will only be available for use in relation to documents capable of being filed electronically. Thus, while the introduction of Statements of Truth has been welcomed as a first step, the need for even more comprehensive reform remains.[316]

315. *See* s.. 21(4) provides that a person who makes a statement of truth without an honest belief as to the truth of that statement shall be guilty of an offence, notwithstanding the law regarding contempt of court. Pursuant to s. 21(5), the statutory penalties for such an offence are: (a) on summary conviction, to a class A fine or to imprisonment for a term not exceeding twelve months, or both, or (b) on conviction on indictment, to a fine not exceeding EUR 250,000 or imprisonment for a term not exceeding five years, or both.

316. *See*, for example, https://www.irishlegal.com/article/flor-mccarthy-campaign-for-statements-of-truth-in-personal-injury-and-medical-negligence-claims-continues (accessed 17 Jan. 2021). *See also* https://www.lawsociety.ie/gazette/top-stories/statements-of-truth-should-have-wider-application-in-law--oboyle/ (accessed 17 Jan. 2021).

Chapter 5. Professional Secrecy

159. The law of evidence requires that, as a general policy, a witness must answer all relevant questions put to him or her.[317] However, pursuant to the so-called doctrine of privilege, in certain situations, particular rights may allow a person to refuse to do so. Sacerdotal privilege, a type of private privilege, allows priests to refuse to answer questions relating to what was said in the confessional.[318] In an Irish context, this privilege, particularly as it relates to information on potential child abuse cases, has proved especially controversial.

160. Confirming the existence of sacerdotal privilege under Irish law in *Cook v. Carroll* in 1945, Duffy J held that there were four core elements in testing for the presence of privilege.[319] First, the communications must originate in confidence that they will not be disclosed. Second, this element of confidentiality must be essential to the full and satisfactory maintenance of the relation. Third, the relation must be one which, in the opinion of the community, should be carefully fostered. Fourth, the injury which would enure to the relation by the disclosure of the communications must be greater than the benefit thereby gained for the correct disposal of litigation. Since then, various cases have applied this test, sometimes expanding on the situations where it may be found to apply.[320]

161. However, the applicability of the privilege in certain circumstances has recently been challenged by legislative developments in Ireland. In 2011, the General Scheme of the Withholding of Information on Offences against Children and Vulnerable Persons Bill was published. The General Scheme drew strong criticism

---

317. *See* Caroline Fennell, *The Law of Evidence in Ireland* (4th ed., Bloomsbury, 2019).
318. For historical analyses of sacerdotal privilege, *see* Walter J. Walsh, 'The Priest-Penitent Privilege: An Hibernocentric Essay in Postcolonial Jurisprudence' 80 *Indiana Law Journal* 1037–1089 (2005).
319. [1945] IR 515. In this regard, he drew on John Henry Wigmore, *A Treatise on the Anglo-American System of Evidence in Trials at Common Law* 2380–2391 (Boston: Little Brown, 3rd ed., 1940) and the so-called Wigmore criteria.
320. In *ER v. JR* [1981] ILRM 125, Carroll J held that communications made to a minister of religion who was acting as a marriage counsellor were privileged. This effectively ensured that sacerdotal privilege applied outside the confessional also. For analysis of *Cook v. Carroll* and developments since then, *see* Bryan McMahon, '"People v. Philips" in Light of Contemporary Developments in Ireland and the U. S.' 11 *American Journal of Irish Studies* 89–110 (2014). *See also Johnston v. Church of Scientology* [2001] 1 IR 682; *Forristal v. Forristal and O'Connor* (1966) 100 ILTR 182. In light of these precedents, the then Ombudsman for Children, Emily Logan, noted in 2011: 'it may very well be that: a priest will have a reasonable excuse for withholding information obtained in the confessional, whether or not the confessor seeks to waive privilege; a priest will have a reasonable excuse for withholding information obtained in confidence outside the confessional, unless this has been waived by the persons confiding; and a secular counsellor may have a reasonable excuse for withholding information obtained in confidence, unless this has been waived by the persons being counselled'. *See Advice of the Ombudsman for Children on the Draft General Scheme for the Criminal Justice (Withholding Information on Crimes Against Children and Vulnerable Adults) Bill 2011,* 3.43 (October 2011).

from the Office of the Ombudsman for Children in appearing to retain sacerdotal privilege, thereby permitting priests to refuse to divulge any confidential communication made to them.[321] The Ombudsman's Office recommended that the issue be clarified and that 'sacerdotal privilege and counsellor privilege should not provide a reasonable excuse for withholding information, given the serious nature of arrestable offences against children'.[322] Notwithstanding the possible constitutional implications of denying the privilege to religious ministers, particularly in light of the protection of religious freedom ensured in Article 44, the Office of the Ombudsman for Children reiterated its belief that it would not be unconstitutional for the legislation to be extended to the confessional and recommended that it 'should be clarified that sacerdotal privilege in respect of communications outside the confessional cannot give rise to a reasonable excuse'.[323] Although on the subsequent publication of the Criminal Justice (Withholding of Information on Offences Against Children and Vulnerable Persons) Bill 2012, the Office of the Ombudsman noted that the Bill was 'clearer than the Scheme that preceded it', it still did not provide 'substantial guidance on what a reasonable excuse for failing to report would be' and appeared to continue to retain sacerdotal privilege.[324]

162. Today, section 2(1) of the Criminal Justice (Withholding of Information on Offences Against Children and Vulnerable Persons) Act 2012 provides that a person shall be guilty of an offence if:

> (a) he or she knows or believes that an offence, that is a Schedule 1 offence, has been committed by another person against a child, and
> (b) he or she has information which he or she knows or believes might be of material assistance in securing the apprehension, prosecution or conviction of that other person for that offence,
>
> and fails without reasonable excuse to disclose that information as soon as it is practicable to do so to a member of the Garda Síochána.[325]

321. *See Advice of the Ombudsman for Children on the Draft General Scheme for the Criminal Justice (Withholding Information on Crimes Against Children and Vulnerable Adults) Bill 2011* (October 2011).
322. *See Advice of the Ombudsman for Children on the Draft General Scheme for the Criminal Justice (Withholding Information on Crimes Against Children and Vulnerable Adults) Bill 2011,* 3.45 (October 2011). For arguments in favour of retaining the privilege, *see* Dáire A.J.L. McCormack-George, 'Sacerdotal Privilege in Irish Law' 33(7) *Irish Law Times* 104 (2015).
323. *See Advice of the Ombudsman for Children on the Draft General Scheme for the Criminal Justice (Withholding Information on Crimes Against Children and Vulnerable Adults) Bill 2011,* 3.54 (October 2011). At 3.52, it noted, 'in the view of the Ombudsman for Children's Office the benefit to the community of maintaining the confessional is not outweighed by the potential danger to children of withholding information'.
324. In *Advice of the Ombudsman for Children on the Heads of the Children First Bill 2012 & The Criminal Justice (Withholding of Information on Offences Against Children and Vulnerable Persons) Bill 2012* (June 2012) privilege is considered at 3.44–3.46.
325. *See also* s. 3(1). For consideration of these provisions, *see* Thomas O'Malley, *Sexual Offences* 291–297 (2nd ed., Roundhall, 2013).

163. Section 2(4), however, provides: 'This section is without prejudice to any right or privilege that may arise in any criminal proceedings by virtue of any rule of law or other enactment entitling a person to refuse to disclose information.'[326]

164. Notwithstanding the apparent legislative intent, as expressed by the then Minister for Justice, Alan Shatter, that mandatory reporting would 'apply regardless of any internal rules of any religious grouping,'[327] it has been noted the legislative language is 'somewhat vague'.[328] O'Malley notes:

> The legislature has … left it to the courts to decide whether any particular privilege applies in specific cases. As the law now stands, it appears that sacerdotal privilege in the strict sense of privilege attaching to the relationship between priest and penitent in the confessional, is absolute and incapable of waiver.[329]

165. Whatever the position of sacerdotal privilege under the 2012 Act, it is important to note that pursuant to Schedule 2 of the Children First Act 2015, 'mandated' persons on whom there is a statutory duty to report suspicions, knowledge or a risk of a child being abused to the Child and Family Agency, expressly includes any 'member of the clergy (howsoever described) or pastoral care worker (howsoever described) of a church or other religious community'.

166. Despite these legal obligations on ministers of religion, guidelines published by the National Board for Safeguarding Children in the Catholic Church in 2018 appeared to advise priests not to inform State authorities about incidents of child abuse they hear about in the confession box, in potential contravention of the law.[330] In light of the controversy this generated, the National Board for Safeguarding Children in the Catholic Church subsequently clarified and amended its guidelines highlighting that it was merely referring to the discrepancy between canon law and civil law and did not intend to advise priests against reporting allegations heard

326. *See also* s. 3(4).
327. *See* 'Child protection measures apply regardless of religious rules' (BBC, 29 Aug. 2011).
328. Liz Heffernan (with Úna Ní Raifeathaigh), *Evidence in Criminal Trials* 731–732 (Bloomsbury Professional, 2014).
329. Thomas O'Malley, *Sexual Offences* 14-09 (2nd ed., Roundhall, 2013). He also states: 'Public discussion prior to the introduction of the 2012 Act was largely dominated by questions about sacerdotal privilege … In all probability this issue will seldom arise in practice … Priestly privilege may also arise in a counselling relationship, but that privilege belongs to the person being counselled and he or she may waive it.' Others, however, have suggested that the 2012 Act does not allow for confessional privilege, *see*, for example, Lydia Buckley, 'Can the Criminal Law Put an End to the "Cover-Up" of Clerical Sexual Abuse?' 24(4) *Irish Criminal Law Journal* 98, 102 (2014).
330. Justine McCarthy, 'Priests Told Not to Report Confessions of Child Abuse by National Board for Safeguarding Children in the Catholic Church' *The Sunday Times*, 12 May 2018. The National Board for Safeguarding Children is a body set up by the Catholic Church to oversee child protection policies.

in confession.[331] As a result, priests are obliged under Irish law to report any allegations of child abuse heard in the confessional to An Garda Síochána (the Irish Police Force), notwithstanding that under canon law, this could cause an excommunication latae sententiae for the priest.

331. *See* Greg Daly, 'Safeguarding Board Rows Back on Confession Seal Advice' *The Irish Catholic*, 21 Jun. 2018. He noted: 'Quoting the revised paragraph from Safeguarding Children Policy and Standards, the spokesperson continued: "All suspicions, concerns and allegations of child abuse must be reported to the statutory authorities through the reporting procedure outlined in Guidance 2.1A. Canon law requires that there is an exception to this rule, which is if abuse is disclosed during the Sacrament of Reconciliation."'

Chapter 6. Medical Ethics

167. Despite the fact that there is no general protection of the right to conscientious objection in Irish law, it has been observed that 'the issue has been the subject of much discussion'.[332] Recent developments in relation to abortion law have placed the issue of conscientious objection, in particular, under the spotlight in both public and academic discourse.

168. The introduction of abortion in Ireland has had a long and controversial history. Although abortion was criminalised under sections 58 and 59 of the Offences Against the Person Act 1861, and this legislation appeared to survive the introduction of the 1937 Irish Constitution, it was not entirely clear what precise implications, if any, the Constitution had on the law in the area.[333] Given this lack of clarity, following a referendum in 1983, a new Article 40.3.3° was inserted into the Constitution, the so-called. It stated:

> The State acknowledges the right to life of the unborn and, with due regard to the equal right to life of the mother, guarantees in its laws to respect, and, as far as practicable, by its laws to defend and vindicate that right.

169. In the intervening years, the prohibition on abortion gave rise to controversial and high-profile cases, none more so than in the *Attorney General v. X* in 1992.[334] There, the Supreme Court took the view that abortion was allowed under the Constitution where: (a) there was a real and substantial risk to the life, as distinct from the health, of the mother; and (b) that risk could only be avoided by the termination of her pregnancy.[335] 'Risk to life' was deemed to include the risk of suicide. In all other circumstances, abortion continued to be unavailable in the jurisdiction.

170. The issue remained to the fore in both public and academic discourse throughout the 1990s and the first decades of the twenty-first century, culminating in the repeal of the Eighth Amendment following a referendum in 2018. The Health (Regulation of Termination of Pregnancy) Act 2018 was subsequently introduced to give legislative effect to the result stating that abortion services may be provided in Ireland in three core situations: where there is a risk to the life or of serious harm

332. Claire Bruton BL & Sarah O'Mahoney BL, 'Religious Discrimination and Expression of Religion: Manifestation of Religious Beliefs in the Workplace' 10(2) *Irish Employment Law Journal* 46, 49 (2013) note 'conscientious objection will arise in the context of potential indirect discrimination claims on grounds of religion or belief only as there is no free-standing right to protection for any such actions taken by employees'.
333. *See G v. An Bord Uchtála* [1980] IR 32 at 69.
334. [1992] 1 IR 1.
335. The case concerned a 14-year-old girl who became pregnant as a result of rape.

to the health of the pregnant woman;[336] where there is a condition likely to lead to the death of foetus;[337] or in early pregnancy, not exceeding twelve weeks' gestation.[338]

171. A key issue, both prior to the 2018 referendum and in its aftermath, concerned the inclusion or otherwise of a conscientious objection clause in any legislation facilitating more permissive regulation of abortion in Ireland. To this end, section 23 of the Health (Regulation of Termination of Pregnancy) Act 2018 now provides for conscientious objection in the context of abortion services provision. Section 23(1) states that nothing in the Act 'shall be construed as obliging any medical practitioner, nurse or midwife to carry out, or to participate in carrying out, a termination of pregnancy' under the legislation to which he or she has a conscientious objection.[339] Pursuant to section 23(3), 'A person who has a conscientious objection ... shall, as soon as may be, make such arrangements for the transfer of care of the pregnant woman concerned as may be necessary to enable the woman to avail of the termination of pregnancy concerned.'[340]

172. The ethical concerns associated with embryonic stem cell research have also 'been the source of great debate' internationally in recent decades.[341] Although

---

336. Section 10(1) provides: '(1) A termination of pregnancy may be carried out in accordance with this section where 2 medical practitioners, having examined the pregnant woman, are of the reasonable opinion formed in good faith that–

   (a) there is a risk to the life, or of serious harm to the health, of the pregnant woman;
   (b) the foetus has not reached viability; and
   (c) it is appropriate to carry out the termination of pregnancy in order to avert the risk referred to in paragraph (a).'

   See also s. 11.

337. Section 12(1) provides: 'A termination of pregnancy may be carried out in accordance with this section where 2 medical practitioners, having examined the pregnant woman, are of the reasonable opinion formed in good faith that there is present a condition affecting the foetus that is likely to lead to the death of the foetus either before, or within 28 days of, birth.'

338. Section 13(1) provides: 'A termination of pregnancy may be carried out in accordance with this section by a medical practitioner where, having examined the pregnant woman, he or she is of the reasonable opinion formed in good faith that the pregnancy concerned has not exceeded 12 weeks of pregnancy.'

339. Note, this does not appear to apply to emergency situations, *see* s. 23(2) and s. 11. Furthermore, the Irish Human Rights and Equality Commission has recommended that provisions governing conscientious objection, and related obligations to refer a pregnant woman to an alternative care provider, should cover a broader range of health and social care professionals than is currently allowed for, *see* https://www.ihrec.ie/human-rights-and-equality-commission-calls-for-conscientious-objection-and-access-provisions-to-be-clearly-set-out-in-abortion-legislation/ (accessed 28 Aug. 2019).

340. Note, the mandatory duty to refer has proved equally controversial, *see* Simon Carswell, 'Anti-abortion GPs Want Protection If They Refuse to Refer Patients' *Irish Times,* 28 May 2018. For a consideration of the arguments for and against conscientious objection clauses, *see* Thomas Finegan, 'Conscientious Objection to Referrals' 45(4) *Journal of Medical Ethics* 277 (2019); cf. Christopher Cowley, 'Conscientious Objection in Healthcare and the Duty to Refer' 43(4) *Journal of Medical Ethics* 207 (2017).

341. Ciara Staunton, '"It's about Actually Having a Proactive Regulatory Framework Versus a Reactive One": Stakeholder Perspectives on the Governance of Embryonic Stem Cell Research in Ireland' 24(2) *Medico-Legal Journal of Ireland* 97 (2018).

there appears to be no constitutional barrier to embryonic stem cell research in Ireland,[342] the development of such research in the jurisdiction has been stunted by the lack of comprehensive legislation on assisted reproduction and associated research to date.[343] While the publication of the Health (Assisted Human Reproduction) Bill 2022 speaks to a legislative intention to legislate for such issues in certain circumstances, it remains to be seen to what extent such research will ultimately be permitted[344] and whether any conscientious objection clauses will be incorporated in any resulting legislation.[345]

173. Beyond conscientious objection clauses, medical ethics and religion have found expression in other areas of Irish law. Pursuant to section 2(1) of the Criminal Justice (Female Genital Mutilation) Act 2012, 'A person is guilty of an offence if the person does or attempts to do an act of female genital mutilation.'[346] Section 2(3) adds: 'it shall not be a defence … for the accused person to show that he or she believed that the act concerned was consented to by the girl concerned or her parents or guardian … or required or permitted for customary or ritual reasons'. Pursuant to section 3(1), it is also a criminal offence to remove a girl from the State where one of the purposes for the removal is to have an act of female genital mutilation done to her. Those found guilty of an offence under the 2012 Act are liable to receive a fine or imprisonment for up to fourteen years or both. In January 2020, the first convictions were recorded under the legislation when a married couple were convicted of the female genital mutilation of their daughter. Judge Elma Sheahan in Dublin Circuit Criminal Court sentenced the father to five and a half years' imprisonment and the mother to four years and nine months' imprisonment.[347]

174. While at present, there is no legislation specifically addressing non-therapeutic male circumcision in Ireland, those performing such procedures are

342. *Roche v. Roche* [2010] 2 IR 321.
343. Ciara Staunton, '"It's about Actually Having a Proactive Regulatory Framework Versus a Reactive One": Stakeholder Perspectives on the Governance of Embryonic Stem Cell Research in Ireland' 24(2) *Medico-Legal Journal of Ireland* 97 (2018) notes that the biggest funders of science in Ireland, namely the Science Foundation Ireland and the Health Research Board, 'have been instructed by the Department of Health since 2009 not to fund [Embryonic and Stem Cell Research] until legislation is introduced'.
344. *See* Part 3 and Sch. 2 of the 2022 Bill.
345. Note, in the United Kingdom, s. 38 of the Human Fertilisation and Embryology Act 1990 includes such a clause in relation to scientific experiments on human foetal tissue. Although not related to medical ethics, on the commencement of the Civil Partnership and Certain Rights and Obligations of Cohabitants Act 2010 calls from certain Catholic civil registrars for exemptions from same-sex ceremonies were widely criticised, *see*, http://www.paschaldonohoe.ie/?p=2752 (2009) (accessed 24 Jul. 2019). *See also* Siobhan Mullally & Darren O'Donovan, 'Religion and Ireland's "Public Squares": Education, the Family and Expanding Equality Claims' (April) *Public Law* 284, 300–306 (2011).
346. Certain exceptions are included in s. 2(2) where, for example, the act concerned is a surgical operation performed by a registered medical practitioner for the protection of the girl/woman's physical or mental health or is completed in connection with labour or birth.
347. 'Parents Jailed over Female Genital Mutilation of Daughter' *Irish Times*, 27 Jan. 2020.

liable to criminal prosecution. In May 2020, a man was jailed by Judge Keenan Johnson in Longford Circuit Criminal Court for three years for carrying out a 'barbaric' circumcision on a baby boy.[348]

348. A further charge under s. 41.b of the Medical Practitioners Act 2007 for falsely representing himself as a medical practitioner was struck out. *See* Tom Tuite, 'Man Jailed for Three Years for "barbaric" Circumcision Without Anaesthetic' *Irish Times*, 25 May 2020. For earlier precedents and discussion, *see* Máiread Enright, 'Whither White Western Values? Comparative Perspectives on Culturally Motivated Decision-Making for the Child' 7(1) *Hibernian Law Journal* 1–16 (2007).

Chapter 7. Non-discrimination

§1. Introduction

175. As noted in earlier parts, Article 40.1 of the Irish Constitution carries a general equality guarantee for citizens. It states: 'All citizens shall, as human persons, be held equal before the law.' However, this guarantee is subject to important qualifications and does not preclude the State from having 'due regard to differences of capacity, physical and moral, and of social function' in its enactments. While the impact of this provision and the case law arising from it is discussed elsewhere in this monograph,[349] this chapter will focus on the legislative initiatives to prevent discrimination. In particular, it will consider the Employment Equality Act 1998 (as amended) and the Equal Status Act 2000 (as amended), which prohibit discrimination on specific, enumerated grounds, including religion and race (which itself includes nationality and ethnicity). Such discrimination cannot arise in employment, vocational training, advertising, collective agreements or in the provision of goods and services.[350]

§2. Equal Status Act 2000 (as Amended)

176. Pursuant to section 5(1) of the Equal Status Act 2000 (as amended), a person shall not discriminate in the disposal of goods or the provision of services. This prohibition encompasses: professional or trade services; health services; access to accommodation and education; facilities for banking, transport and cultural activities.[351] As regards the burden of proof, the complainant must first establish a prima facie case of discriminatory treatment. When this has been established, the burden of proof shifts to the respondent to rebut the presumption of discrimination.[352] Four types of discrimination are recognised under section 3(1) of the 2000 Act (as amended): direct discrimination;[353] indirect discrimination;[354] discrimination by association;[355] and discrimination by imputation.[356] Ten discriminatory grounds are recognised in section 3(2), with the 'religion ground' located in section 3(2)(e).

349. *See* Part II and Part IX in particular.

350. Note, the Irish Human Rights and Equality Commission provides information and advice to persons who feel that they have been discriminated against under the legislation, whether in relation to employment equality or equal status. *See* Part V Ch. 1 for more on the Commission.

351. However, exceptions do exist, *see* below.

352. *See* s. 38A(1) of the Equal Status Act 2000 (as amended).

353. To establish direct discrimination, a direct comparison must be made. For example, in the case of alleged religious discrimination, a comparison must be made between persons of different religious persuasions or between a person who is a member of a religious denomination and another who is not.

354. Pursuant to s. 3(1)(c) of the Equal Status Act 2000 (as amended), indirect discrimination occurs when seemingly neutral practices or policies nevertheless have a discriminatory impact. It might arise where an individual or group of people are placed at a disadvantage as a result of conditions or rules which they would find hard to satisfy and which cannot be reasonably justified.

355. Discrimination by association is covered by s. 3(1)(b) of the Equal Status Act 2000 (as amended) and arises when a person is treated less favourably due to their association with or connection to another person.

177. However, despite its apparent breadth, general and specific derogations are included, which, in certain circumstances, effectively permit discrimination on the religion ground. Thus, under section 5(2)(e), this prohibition on discrimination does not apply where people are treated differently on the basis of their religion in relation to goods or services provided for a religious purpose. Section 6(5) also permits the reservation of premises or accommodation for the exclusive use of persons in a particular category for a religious purpose. Notwithstanding that discrimination by clubs is prohibited under section 8, section 9 adds that where the principal purpose of the club is to cater only for the needs of, for example, persons of a particular religious belief, nationality or ethnic or national origin, a club shall not be considered to be discriminating. Important exemptions also apply in relation to the provision of education, as discussed further in Part IX Chapter 2.

178. Section 3(2)(j) of the Equal Status Act 2000 (as amended) provides protection against victimisation. The 'victimisation ground' may arise where one has, in good faith, applied for any determination or redress under the Act, has attended as a witness in connection with any inquiry or proceedings under the Act, has given evidence in any criminal proceedings under this Act, has opposed by lawful means an act which is unlawful under this Act or has given notice of an intention to take any of these actions and is discriminated as a result.

179. Sexual and other harassment are addressed in section 11 of the Equal Status Act 2000 (as amended). It places an onus on service providers to protect against harassment, defined as 'any form of unwanted conduct related to any of the discriminatory grounds',[357] including the religion ground. Such unwanted conduct may consist of acts, requests, spoken words, gestures or the production, display or circulation of written words, pictures or other material.[358] Section 11(2) effectively makes the person in charge of the location where the harassment is occurring vicariously liable for the harassment or sexual harassment.[359] This means that they are responsible for making sure that anyone who has a right to be on their premises is not subject to harassment or sexual harassment, and it places the onus on them to prevent it from happening.[360]

---

356. Section 3(1)(a)(iv) of the Equal Status Act 2000 (as amended) provides for discrimination by imputation. This may arise where a person is treated less favourably due to a belief that they belong to one of the categories covered by the enumerated grounds, whether or not that is the case.
357. Section 5(a)(i) of the Equal Status Act 2000 (as amended).
358. Section 5(b) of the Equal Status Act 2000 (as amended).
359. Section 11(2) of the Equal Status Act 2000 (as amended) provides:

> A person ('the responsible person') who is responsible for the operation of any place that is an educational establishment or at which goods, services or accommodation facilities are offered to the public shall not permit another person who has a right to be present in or to avail himself or herself of any facilities, goods or services provided at that place, to suffer sexual harassment or harassment at that place.

360. Note, s. 11(3) of the Equal Status Act 2000 (as amended) provides: 'It shall be a defence for the responsible person to prove that he or she took such steps as are reasonably practicable to prevent the sexual harassment or harassment, as the case may be … .'

180. Complaints under the Equal Status Act 2000 (as amended) require the complainant to first notify the person or organisation they are making the complaint against. Such notification must take place within two months of the last act of discrimination.[361] If the service provider has not responded within one month of the date the notification was sent, or in circumstances where the complainant is not satisfied with the response received, they can bring a complaint to the Workplace Relations Commission (WRC) within six months of the last act of discrimination.[362] Appeals under the Acts from the WRC are then dealt with by the Circuit Court.

§3. Employment Equality Act 1998 (As Amended)

181. The Employment Equality Act 1998 (as amended) plays an important role in promoting equality in the context of employment and has been described as providing 'extensive protection from discrimination in employment for those from minority faiths, such as Islam'.[363] Pursuant to section 8(1), the Act outlaws discrimination in relation to recruitment, promotion, pay, working conditions, training or experience and dismissal.[364] Section 6 defines discrimination as treating one person in a less favourable way than another person is, has been or would be treated in a comparable situation on any of the nine grounds specified. Discrimination by imputation is addressed in section 6(1)(a)(iv) of the Employment Equality Act 1998 (as amended) and discrimination by association is covered in section 6(1)(b). The 'religion ground', where one person has a different religious belief from the other, or one has a religious belief, and the other does not, is captured in section 6(2)(e). 'Religious belief' for the purposes of the Act is defined in section 2(1) as including religious background or outlook.[365]

182. However, there are important exceptions to the non-discrimination principle. Section 37(1) of the Employment Equality Act 1998 (as amended) provides that certain religious, educational and medical institutions, whose objectives include the provision of services in an environment which promotes religious values, are not

---

361. *See* Part III of the Equal Status Act 2000 (as amended).

362. The Workplace Relations Commission took over from the Equality Tribunal which previously adjudicated on the Equal Status Acts.

363. Claire Hogan, 'Accommodation of Faith in the Irish Workplace: European and Irish Perspectives' 14(2) *Irish Employment Law Journal* 37, 49 (2017). Note, provisions originally carried in the Refugee Act 1996 and now located in the International Protection Act 2015 (s. 16(3)(b)) which prevented asylum seekers from seeking or entering employment before final determination of their application was found to be unconstitutional, *see NVH v. Minister for Justice & Equality and ors* [2017] IESC 35. Although the decision was not based on equality arguments, the ban on work had adversely affected a number of asylum seekers in Ireland, many of whom represent minority religions.

364. Claire Hogan, 'Accommodation of Faith in the Irish Workplace: European and Irish Perspectives' 14(2) *Irish Employment Law Journal* 37, 48 (2017) notes 'The legislation is wide in scope, prohibiting direct and indirect discrimination in a variety of areas relevant to employment in both the public and private sectors.' *See also* Frances Meenan, *Employment Law* Ch. 12 (Roundhall, 2014); Margaret Bolger, Claire Bruton & Cliona Kimber, *Employment Equality Law* Ch. 9 (Roundhall, 2012).

365. *See Irish Prison Service v. Morris* (EDA4/2007 28 Feb. 2007).

necessarily regarded as engaging in discrimination within the meaning of the Act where they give more favourable treatment on the religion ground to an employee. This exception applies where the treatment is considered reasonable in order to maintain the religious ethos of the institution. Furthermore, it is not discrimination where an employer takes action, which is reasonably necessary to prevent an employee from undermining the religious ethos of that institution.[366]

183. Amendments introduced via the Equality (Miscellaneous Provisions) Act 2015 have sought to constrain the application of the derogation in section 37(1) in the specific context of publicly funded religious, educational or medical institutions. The new provisions are now located in section 37(1A), (1B) and (1C). They provide that in order for such institutions to rely on the derogation permitting favourable treatment on the religion ground to an employee, there must be no other discriminatory ground (such as gender or race) on which the differential treatment would constitute discrimination, and the religion or belief of the employee or prospective employee must constitute 'a genuine, legitimate and justified occupational requirement having regard to the institution's ethos'.[367] To benefit from the exception whereby an employer may take action to prevent an employee from undermining the religious ethos of that institution, section 37(1B) states the action must be objectively justified and the means of achieving that aim are appropriate and necessary. In this regard, a proportionality test set out in section 37(1C) will govern the standard of what is considered justifiable. Any action to protect the institution's ethos will not be considered objectively justified, appropriate and necessary unless it is rationally and strictly related to the institution's religious ethos, is in response to the conduct of the prospective employee rather than membership of another protected category and is proportionate to their conduct.

184. Akin to the provisions in the Equal Status Act 2000 (as amended), section 14A of the Employment Equality Act 1998 (as amended) also prohibits harassment in the workplace. Again, harassment is defined to include 'any form of unwanted conduct' related to any of the discriminatory grounds, for example, religious beliefs, and may consist of spoken words, gestures or the production, display or circulation of written words, pictures or other material that is unwelcome and could reasonably be regarded as offensive, humiliating or intimidating.[368] Complaints under the Employment Equality Act 1998 (as amended) must be brought to the WRC within six months of the last act of discrimination.

366. Section 37(1)(b) of the Employment Equality Act 1998 (as amended). Note also, s. 12 carries derogations for denominations in relation to vocational training. Religious institutions can reserve places on certain teaching and nursing courses in circumstances where the education and health authorities deem this necessary to maintain the proportion of teachers and nurses. This Irish position proved somewhat influential at EU level in the drafting of Council Directive 2000/78/EC, *see* Art. 4(2). For more, *see* Eoin Daly, *Religion, Law and the Irish State* 170 (Clarus, 2012).

367. Section 37(1A).

368. Section 14A(7).

185. While equality legislation such as the Employment Equality Act 1998 (as amended) and the Equal Status Act 2000 (as amended) is undoubtedly to be welcomed in prioritising respect for religious pluralism and diversity, the precise scope of the legislation remains unclear. The 'dearth of case law involving claims for requests for freedom of expression of religions such [as] Islam in the Irish workplace' has been noted.[369] In a similar vein, there also remains an as yet underdeveloped body of case law concerning Irish equality law provisions.[370] It remains to be seen, for example, whether section 37 could be used to justify recruitment or other practices in a post-primary education setting for teachers other than those charged with teaching religion or, indeed, could be used to justify employment decisions in relation to ancillary staff.[371] Equally, whether an institution can discriminate on religious affiliation only or may be permitted to adopt a more liberal interpretation and consider the degree of orthodoxy an employee might express has yet to be clarified in the Superior Courts.

369. Claire Hogan, 'Accommodation of Faith in the Irish Workplace: European and Irish Perspectives' 14(2) *Irish Employment Law Journal* 37, 45 (2017). *See also* Claire Hogan, 'The Accommodation of Islam in the Irish Workplace, Classroom and Hospital' in Kathryn O'Sullivan (ed.) *Minority Religions under Irish Law: Islam in National and International Context* 83–107 (Brill, 2019).

370. A prospective case involving a Sikh complainant who was informed that he could not wear his turban as part of the Garda Reserve uniform failed to materialise given he was not regarded as an 'employee' within the meaning of the Employment Equality Act 1998 (as amended), *see Ravinder Singh Oberoi v. Commissioner of An Garda Síochána* [2013] IEHC 267; [2014] 25 ELR 17.

371. *See* Eoin Daly, *Religion, Law and the Irish State* 167–168 (Clarus, 2012).

Chapter 8. Penal Law and Religion

§1. Introduction

186. There are various ways in which penal law and religion continue to interact in Ireland, notwithstanding that 'religious offences', per se, are not expressly referenced in Irish statutes. As Colton notes: 'Religion exists in twenty-first century Ireland in a more widely articulated and all-encompassing statutory framework than that of previous eras when specific crimes against religion were delineated.'[372] Some of the more obvious interactions, such as the former criminalisation of blasphemy, have received attention elsewhere in this monograph.[373] This chapter, however, seeks to briefly highlight the particular issues arising in relation to offences protecting religious worship and hate crimes.

§2. Offences Protecting Religious Worship

187. Reflecting on the 'clear shift' in Irish legislation and policy, Colton explains:

> Crimes which specifically enunciate offences against religion as an institution, and against the officials and property of religious institutions have, for the most part, been superseded by statutory offences widely articulated within the generality of the criminal law and designed to protect instead individuals who hold religious beliefs and their freedom to adhere to such beliefs.[374]

188. In this regard, offences protecting religious worship have undergone reform. Although historically, pursuant to section 36 of the Offences Against the Person Act 1861, it was an offence to obstruct an ordained person on their way to take a religious service, protection against such infringements is now considered to fall within the broader remit of the Non-Fatal Offences Against the Person Act 1997 (as amended). Similarly, while the crime of sacrilege – defined as breaking into a 'place of divine worship' and committing any felony – was recognised pursuant to the Larceny Act 1861 and the Larceny Act 1916, this was replaced by the broader crime of burglary under the Criminal Law (Jurisdiction) Act 1976.[375] The protection of cemeteries and churchyards now also falls under general legislation directed

372. Paul Colton, 'Religion and Criminal Law in Ireland' in Norman Doe & Matti Kotiranta (eds) *Religion and Criminal Law in Member States of the EU, Proceedings of the European Consortium for Church and State Research* (Peteers, 2013).
373. *See* Part VII Ch. 3.
374. Paul Colton, 'Religion and Criminal Law in Ireland' in Norman Doe & Matti Kotiranta (eds) *Religion and Criminal Law in Member States of the EU, Proceedings of the European Consortium for Church and State Research* (Peteers, 2013).
375. Note also, the Criminal Justice (Theft and Fraud Offences) Act 2001 (as amended).

at the maintenance of public order.[376] In relation to the protection of the burial of the dead or infringements therewith, it is likely that such violations could be regarded as offences within the common law, notwithstanding the lack of specific legislation on the matter.[377]

189. Several more specifically religious offences are included in the Civil Registration Act 2004 (as amended) in relation to the solemnisation of marriage and carry particular importance for religious solemnisers. For example, section 69(10)(c) of the 2004 Act (as amended) states it is an offence for a person who is a registered solemniser to solemnise a marriage without a Marriage Registration Form (MRF) having been given to him/her before the solemnisation for examination. Various other offences are also enumerated throughout subsection 10 and include solemnising a marriage where the location (section 69(10)(e)) or notification (section 69(10)(f)) requirements have not been met.[378] Moreover, pursuant to section 70(2), a person guilty of an offence under section 69(10) shall be liable on summary conviction to a fine not exceeding EUR 2,000 or imprisonment for a term not exceeding six months or both.[379] Pursuant to section 69(10)(b) of the 2004 Act (as amended), it is also an offence for a person who is not a registered solemniser or holder of temporary authorisation to conduct a marriage ceremony in such a way as to lead the parties to the marriage to believe that he or she is solemnising a valid marriage.

§3. Prohibition of Incitement to Hatred

190. In Ireland, the Prohibition of Incitement to Hatred Act 1989 serves as a statutory prohibition against incitement to hatred on religious grounds. Pursuant to section 1, 'hatred' is as defined as 'hatred against a group of persons in the State or elsewhere on account of their race, colour, nationality, religion, ethnic or national origins, membership of the travelling community or sexual orientation'. Section 2 of the Act provides that it is an offence for a person 'to publish or distribute written material', 'to use words, behave or display written material' in public[380] or 'to distribute, show or play a recording of visual images or sounds' if such material, words, behaviour, images or sounds 'are threatening, abusive or insulting and are intended or, having regard to all the circumstances, are likely to stir up hatred'. Various

376. For more, *see* Paul Colton, 'Religion and Criminal Law in Ireland' in Norman Doe & Matti Kotiranta (eds) *Religion and Criminal Law in Member States of the EU, Proceedings of the European Consortium for Church and State Research* (Peteers, 2013).
377. For the law regarding inquests, specifically, *see* the Coroners Act 1962. Note also, the Coroners Amendment Act 2019.
378. *See* Part X Ch. 1 for more on the formalities for entry into marriage.
379. *See* Kathryn O'Sullivan, 'Religious-Only Marriages and Officiant-Based Marriage Law Reform: An Irish Perspective' 49 *Family Law* 1156 (2019).
380. Section 2(1)(b)(ii) notes it is an offence to also do so 'inside a private residence so that the words, behaviour or material are heard or seen by persons outside the residence'.

defences to a charge are also outlined in the subsection.[381] Further offences are outlined in sections 3 and 4, which pertain to the broadcasting of threatening, abusive or insulting visual images or sounds as well as the preparation or possession of materials which are, for example, threatening or insulting and are intended or are likely to stir up hatred.[382]

191. However, significant attention has been placed on the perceived lack of implementation of the legislation, with the ineffectiveness and inappropriateness of the legislation in addressing the practical reality of hate crime noted by law enforcement agencies.[383] As was recently highlighted, Ireland does not have legislation that requires a court to take a bias motivation or a demonstration of bias into account

---

381. *See* s. 2(2) of the 1989 Act which states:

> (a) In proceedings for an offence under subsection (1), if the accused person is not shown to have intended to stir up hatred, it shall be a defence for him to prove that he was not aware of the content of the material or recording concerned and did not suspect, and had no reason to suspect, that the material or recording was threatening, abusive or insulting.
> (b) In proceedings for an offence under subsection (1) (b), it shall be a defence for the accused person–
>   (i) to prove that he was inside a private residence at the relevant time and had no reason to believe that the words, behaviour or material concerned would be heard or seen by a person outside the residence, or
>   (ii) if he is not shown to have intended to stir up hatred, to prove that he did not intend the words, behaviour or material concerned to be, and was not aware that they might be, threatening, abusive or insulting.

382. Section 4(1) of the Prohibition of the Incitement to Hatred Act 1989 provides:

> It shall be an offence for a person–
> (a) to prepare or be in possession of any written material with a view to its being distributed, displayed, broadcast or otherwise published, in the State or elsewhere, whether by himself or another, or
> (b) to make or be in possession of a recording of sounds or visual images with a view to its being distributed, shown, played, broadcast or otherwise published, in the State or elsewhere, whether by himself or another, if the material or recording is threatening, abusive or insulting and is intended or, having regard to all the circumstances, including such distribution, display, broadcasting, showing, playing or other publication thereof as the person has, or it may reasonably be inferred that he has, in view, is likely to stir up hatred.

Defences are again included in s. 4(2). Section 4(3) adds that where it is proved that the accused person was in possession of material or a recording referred to in s. 4(1), and where it is 'reasonable to assume that the material or recording was not intended for the personal use of the person', the burden of proof is placed on the accused to prove his or her possession of the material or recording is not in contravention of s. 4(1).

383. Note, having searched all major legal databases for reported cases involving the Prohibition of Incitement to Hatred Act 1989, recent research found only one such case, *see* Amanda Haynes & Jennifer Schweppe, *Lifecycle of a Hate Crime: Country Report for Ireland* 12 (ICCL, 2017). *See also*, Amanda Haynes et al., *Out of the Shadows: Legislating for Hate Crime in Ireland* 44 (University of Limerick, 2015). For an earlier critique, *see* the National Consultative Committee on Racism and Interculturalism, *Prohibition of Incitement to Hatred Act 1989: A Review* (August 2001).

when determining the appropriate sanction to impose in a given case.[384] While the 1989 Act criminalises incitement to hatred, it has been observed that 'it is aimed at criminalising hate speech and is thus purposefully narrow in its scope and by its nature not suited to addressing hate crime'.[385] The difficulties in adapting the legislation to online platforms have also been highlighted.[386] In this context, in its role as Ireland's national human rights and equality body, the IHREC stated at the end of 2018, 'there is no doubt that the Prohibition of Incitement to Hatred Act 1989 is not fit for purpose and should be modernised'.[387] The need for the introduction of comprehensive and broader hate crime legislation seems particularly urgent.

192. It now appears that reform may be forthcoming. Public consultation on the issue was undertaken by the Department of Justice from November 2019 to January 2020, resulting in the publication of the Legislating for Hate Speech and Hate Crime in Ireland Report.[388] The Criminal Justice (Incitement to Violence or Hatred and Hate Offences) Bill 2022 was subsequently published and is currently making its way through the Oireachtas.

384. *See* Amanda Haynes & Jennifer Schweppe, *Lifecycle of a Hate Crime: Country Report for Ireland* 11 (ICCL, 2017).

385. *See* Amanda Haynes & Jennifer Schweppe, *Lifecycle of a Hate Crime: Country Report for Ireland* 11 (ICCL, 2017). They note: 'In the absence of legislation addressing hate crime, An Garda Síochána overcome the limitations imposed by this lacuna by recording what they refer to as "discriminatory motives" in relation to standard offences. Garda HQ Directive No 04/2007 states that any incident which is perceived by "the victim or another person" – for example the police officer, a witness, or a person acting on behalf of the victim – as having a racist motivation should be recorded as such.'

386. Eugenia Siapera, Elena Moreo & Jiang Zhou, *Hate Track: Tracking and Monitoring Racist Speech Online* (DCU, 2018) highlighted that '[w]hile the Act is technically broad enough to include online offences, there are difficulties in adapting current legislation to online platforms; to date, public shaming and media outrage, rather than legal sanctions, have been the typical response to racist online utterances in Ireland as elsewhere'.

387. 'Human Rights and Equality Commission Challenges Rise of Hate Speech Online' (28 Nov. 2018) available at https://www.ihrec.ie/human-rights-and-equality-commission-challenges-rise-of-hate-speech-online/ (accessed 28 Aug. 2019).

388. https://assets.gov.ie/237922/07cb2005-2712-4808-9b48-348f224806b5.pdf (accessed 29 Feb. 2024).

Part VIII. Church Financing

Chapter 1. Direct Financing of Religious Communities

193. As noted elsewhere in this monograph, at a legal and constitutional level, Church-State relations in Ireland are markedly separationist when compared with the other EU Member States. In this context, Ireland is one of only three jurisdictions in the EU that prohibit State endowment of religions.[389] A prohibition on the State endowment of any religion is included in Article 44.2.2° of the Irish Constitution, which simply provides that 'The State guarantees not to endow any religion.' Although on direct reading, the ban on endowment might seem absolute, the precise meaning of 'endowment' has been qualified by the Irish courts. In particular, as Daly notes, '[t]he sole Supreme Court ruling to have issued an authoritative interpretation of the endowment clause has significantly restricted its scope, at least in terms of its application to public education'.[390]

194. In Campaign to *Separate Church and State v. Minister for Education*, the Supreme Court considered the meaning of 'endowment'.[391] Despite holding that the State's funding of Roman Catholic and Church of Ireland chaplaincy services in the community and comprehensive schools did constitute 'endowment', the court nevertheless found that such endowment was justified since it was for education that can be religious.[392] In short, the court found that the payment effectively constituted support for education. Viewed in light of Article 44 of the Irish Constitution, Barrington J concluded that parents who chose such secondary schools enjoyed a 'right to have religious education provided in the schools which their children attend'.[393] This right then provided constitutional legitimacy for the State's payment of chaplains' salaries.[394]

389. The others being France and the Netherlands. Thus, although there is no prohibition on the establishment of a recognised church in Ireland as noted in Part III Ch. 1, this prohibition on the State endowment of any religious denomination effectively achieves this end.

390. Eoin Daly, 'Re-evaluating the Purpose of Church-State Separation in the Irish Constitution: The Endowment Clause as a Protection of Religious Freedom and Equality' 2 *Judicial Studies Institute Journal* 86, 87 (2008). He suggests at 86 that Art. 44.2.2° 'may be regarded as one of the most under-exploited provisions of the Constitution'.

391. [1998] 3 IR 321.

392. *See* the right to religious education carried in Art. 44 discussed in Part IX.

393. *Campaign to Separate Church and State v. Minister for Education* [1998] 3 IR 321, 358.

394. *See* Eoin Daly, *Religion, Law and the Irish State* 320–370 (Clarus, 2012); Oran Doyle, 'Article 44: Privileging the Rights of the Religious' in Eoin Carolan & Oran Doyle (eds) *The Irish Constitution: Governance and Values* 476, 483–485 (Roundhall, 2008). *See also Re Article 26 and the*

195. The extent to which State support for the provision of chaplaincy services beyond primary or secondary education may be constitutionally justifiable remains open to question, however. On the one hand, as Daly has highlighted, funding for chaplaincies in the context of the armed forces 'is likely justified on the grounds that an all-encompassing military life … would otherwise deprive members of the opportunity to practice religion'.[395] Such logic would also likely justify financial aid for prison chaplains.[396] On the other hand, he notes, '[t]he provision of chaplaincy services in higher education institutions … is far more vulnerable'.[397] He argues that 'the use of public funds for university chaplaincies could not be considered qualitatively different, constitutionally speaking, from the hypothetical sponsorship of religious activities for employees in state agencies'.[398] He concludes, however, that such support may be justified on the basis of pastoral care.[399]

196. Although State financial assistance for religious organisations in Ireland is limited,[400] congregations associated with the Roman Catholic Church have benefitted in recent times from what has been described as 'a blank cheque' from the Irish State.[401] In 2002, following the Commission to Inquire into Child Abuse (the so-called Ryan Commission), an Indemnity Agreement was reached between the Irish Government and religious congregations. It saw eighteen Roman Catholic religious congregations benefit from a State indemnity against all future actions by people who, as children, had been in institutions run by them. In return for this indemnity, the organisations pledged to contribute EUR 128 million. While this figure may seem significant, the Irish State has incurred costs in excess of EUR 1.4 billion arising from the abuse to date. Doubts have been raised as to the constitutionality of the indemnity agreement, and the issue continues to cause controversy in public discourse.[402]

Employment Equality Bill 1996 [1997] 2 IR 321, at 354 for consideration of Art. 44.2.2° and the potential acceptability of concurrent 'endowment' of all religions. *See* Eoin Daly, 'Re-evaluating the Purpose of Church-State Separation in the Irish Constitution: The Endowment Clause as a Protection of Religious Freedom and Equality' 2 *Judicial Studies Institute Journal* 86 (2008) for further discussion.

395. Eoin Daly, *Religion, Law and the Irish State* 372 (Clarus, 2012). He notes, 'religious freedom would trump any concerns arising from non-endowment (the potentially discriminatory or sectarian nature of services provided may be another matter)'.
396. *See* Part XI Ch. 3 for more.
397. Eoin Daly, *Religion, Law and the Irish State* 372 (Clarus, 2012).
398. Eoin Daly, *Religion, Law and the Irish State* 372–373 (Clarus, 2012).
399. Eoin Daly, *Religion, Law and the Irish State* 372–373 (Clarus, 2012).
400. Note Part VI above regarding the payment of State pensions to clergy providing services to the public.
401. *See* Patsy McGarry, 'Religious Congregations Indemnity Deal Was "a Blank Cheque", Says Michael McDowell' *Irish Times*, 5 Apr. 2019.
402. *See* Eoin Daly, *Religion, Law and the Irish State* 373–379 (Clarus, 2012). He concludes: 'The 2002 Act was not in itself unconstitutional, but the indemnity, as an administrative action whose purpose, object and effect was to benevolently assume the legal costs of the religious orders, demonstrably was.' *See also* Eoin Daly, 'The Congregational Indemnity Agreement: An Unconstitutional Endowment of Religion?' 27 *Irish Law Times* 111 (2009).

197. Finally, unlike other European countries, Ireland does not apply any system of church tax or equivalent. As such organisations are self-supporting, voluntary donations remain an important source of funding.

Chapter 2. Indirect Financing of Religious Communities

198. As noted above, although certain State payments might appear to be endowing a religion with direct financial aid, where provided for the delivery of public service, such payments may be constitutionally justifiable as a means of serving a secular need and conferring a mere indirect financial benefit on the religious denomination concerned. Such indirect endowment to certain religions or religious representatives playing the role of a service provider is most evident in the context of education and in the payment of chaplains.[403]

199. Indirect financial assistance may also be available through various general State funds. For example, religious organisations may apply for funding under the LEADER Programme 2023–2027, which is administered by the Department of Rural and Community Development.[404] LEADER is a European funding initiative involved in local development with organisations including the Church of Ireland benefitting from grants for building works that fall into relevant criteria, such as the upgrading of rural heritage and renewal and development works.[405] Funding may also be available under the Historic Structures Fund and Built Heritage Investment Scheme administered by the Department for Housing, Local Government and Heritage.

200. Finally, religious organisations may benefit from tax exemptions where they have secured official Charitable Tax Exemption status.[406] Religious bodies who are registered as charities may be exempt from paying a range of different taxes, including Income Tax, Corporation Tax, Capital Gains Tax, Deposit Interest Retention Tax, Capital Acquisitions Tax, Dividend Withholding Tax and Stamp Duty. Tax relief may also be claimed by charities on donations made to them.[407]

---

403. In this context, Eoin Daly, *Religion, Law and the Irish State* 319 (Clarus, 2012) notes that Art. 44.2.2° continues to give significant latitude to the State in its arrangements with religions.
404. *See*, https://www.pobal.ie/programmes/leader-programme-2023-2027/ (accessed 1 Nov. 2023).
405. *See*, https://www.ireland.anglican.org/cmsfiles/pdf/Resources/ParishResources/Finance/Main-Sources-of-Church-Grants.pdf (accessed 28 Aug. 2019).
406. *See*, http://www.revenue.ie/en/about/publications/charities_alpha.pdf (accessed 26 May 2017).
407. For consideration of the extent to which Irish law facilitates Sharia-compliant mortgages and financial services, *see* Edana Richardson, 'A Comparative Review of the Accommodation of Islamic Finance in Irish Law' in Kathryn O'Sullivan (ed.) *Minority Religions under Irish Law: Islam in National and International Context* 157 (Brill, 2019).

Part IX. Education

Introduction

201. A large majority of schools in Ireland, despite attracting State funding, are denominational and privately owned and operated. As a result, it has been observed that the Irish education system may be 'best described as a State-aided, as distinct from a State-owned and administered, system of education'.[408] However, although the Roman Catholic Church remains the dominant educational service provider in the jurisdiction, the demand for more multi-denominational or non-denominational schools is growing. The desirability of recognising and encouraging greater diversity in the Irish educational system is also now reflected at a legislative level. Pursuant to section 7(4) of the Education Act 1998 (as amended), in carrying out his or her functions, the Minister for Education is required to have regard to the need to 'reflect the diversity of educational services provided in the State'. Section 10(2)(b) further requires the Minister to have regard to the 'desirability of diversity' in relation to school recognition.

408. Claire Hogan, 'Accommodating Islam in the Denomination Irish Education System' 31(4) *Journal of Muslim Minority Affairs* 554, 555 (2011).

Chapter 1. Religious Education in Public and Private Schools

202. From around 4 to 12 years of age, children in Ireland attend primary school, whether public or private, whether denominational or non-denominational. Post-primary education is then typically delivered to children from 12 to 18 years of age. Pursuant to the Education (Welfare) Act 2000 (as amended), it is the responsibility of parents to ensure that their children attend a recognised school or receive a certain minimum education from the age of 6 to the age of 16 or until they have completed three years of second level of education.[409]

203. The Education Act 1998 (as amended) represents the key legislation in the area and provides the broad framework, objectives and principles underpinning the Irish education system at both primary and post-primary levels.[410] Section 30(1) of the 1998 Act (as amended) provides that the Minister for Education may, following such consultation as deemed appropriate, prescribe the curriculum for recognised schools. This includes the subjects to be offered in recognised schools, the syllabus of each subject, the amount of instruction time to be allotted to each subject, and the guidance and counselling provision to be offered in schools. However, it is made clear in section 30(4) that, provided the curriculum as laid down by the State is taught, a school may provide courses of instruction in such other subjects as it deems appropriate.

204. Schools in Ireland are run by Boards of Management which receive statutory status and recognition under the Education Act 1998 (as amended). Pursuant to section 14(1):

> It shall be the duty of a patron, for the purposes of ensuring that a recognised school is managed in a spirit of partnership, to appoint where practicable a board of management the composition of which is agreed between patrons of schools, national associations of parents, recognised school management organisations, recognised trade unions and staff associations representing teachers and the Minister.

205. With limited exceptions, a Board so established 'shall be a body corporate with perpetual succession and power to sue and may be sued in its corporate name'

409. 'Interpretation' of the Education (Welfare) Act 2000 provides that '"child" means a person resident in the State who has reached the age of 6 years and who– (a) has not reached the age of 16 years, or (b) has not completed 3 years of post-primary education, whichever occurs later, but shall not include a person who has reached the age of 18 years'. Beyond this definition, *see* s. 17 of the Education (Welfare) Act 2000 for the duty of parents regarding the education of their children. The 2000 Act also seeks to address the needs of children and young people who have, or may have, school attendance difficulties.
410. The 1998 Act (as amended) also provides for the rights of children and others to education and clarifies the roles and the responsibilities of teachers, principals, school patrons, Boards of Management and the Minister for Education.

pursuant to section 14(2).[411] Board members are appointed by the patron of the school under section 14(3).[412]

206. Section 15 of the Education Act 1998 (as amended) outlines the responsibilities of the Board of Management.[413] In performing its functions, the Board is explicitly directed to uphold 'the characteristic spirit of the school' as determined by its 'cultural, educational, moral, religious, social, linguistic and spiritual values and traditions'.[414] Moreover, the Board shall publish its admissions policies[415] and shall 'have regard to the principles and requirements of a democratic society and have respect and promote respect for the diversity of values, beliefs, traditions, languages and ways of life in society'.[416] It shall have regard to the efficient use of resources and the public interest in the affairs of the school and shall be accountable to those served by the school.[417] Finally, the Board shall make 'reasonable provision and accommodation for students with a disability or other special educational needs'.[418]

207. The delivery of religious education has also been subject to particular regulatory intervention. For fifty years, religious education at the primary school level in Ireland was informed by Rules 68 and 69 of the 'Rules for National Schools', which were published in 1965.[419] These rules provided that religious instruction was 'by far the most important' part of a school's curriculum and ensured that religious instruction was to be regarded as a priority subject in primary school classrooms. In January 2016, however, these provisions were rescinded by the Minister for Education, with Boards of Management instead directed to simply be guided by section

411. An exception is provided in the case of a school established or maintained by an education and training board.
412. Note, pursuant to s. 14(8): 'Where a patron determines that the appointment of a board in accordance with subsection (1) is not practicable, the patron shall inform the parents of students, the teachers and other staff of the school and the Minister of that fact and the reasons therefor at the time of such determination and, thereafter, if a board is not so appointed, the patron shall, from time to time or as requested by the Minister, inform the parents, teachers and other staff and the Minister of the reasons therefor.'
413. Section 15(1) of the Education Act 1998 (as amended) states: 'It shall be the duty of a board to manage the school on behalf of the patron and for the benefit of the students and their parents and to provide or cause to be provided an appropriate education for each student at the school for which that board has responsibility.'
414. Section 15(2)(b).
415. Section 15(2)(d) provides the board shall 'publish, in such manner as the board with the agreement of the patron considers appropriate, the policy of the school concerning admission to and participation in the school, including the policy of the school relating to the expulsion and suspension of students and admission to and participation by students with disabilities or who have other special educational needs, and ensure that as regards that policy principles of equality and the right of parents to send their children to a school of the parents' choice are respected and such directions as may be made from time to time by the Minister, having regard to the characteristic spirit of the school and the constitutional rights of all persons concerned, are complied with'.
416. Section 15(2)(e).
417. Section 15(2)(f).
418. Section 15(2)(g).
419. *See*, https://www.into.ie/media-centre/circulars/rules-for-national-schools-1965/ (accessed 18 Jan. 2021).

15(2)(b) of the 1998 Act (as amended), thus requiring that religious instruction merely have regard to the 'characteristic spirit' of the school.[420]

208. In early 2023, the Department of Education published its Primary Curriculum Framework For Primary and Special Schools.[421] Representing the first major review of the curriculum in twenty-five years, it reduces time allocated to the teaching of religion from two-and-a-half hours a week to two hours, with the subject now reformulated as part of a new and broader 'religious, ethical, multi-belief and values education' subject on the curriculum.

420. https://circulars.gov.ie/pdf/circular/education/2016/09.pdf (accessed 18 Jan. 2021).
421. *See*, https://www.curriculumonline.ie/getmedia/84747851-0581-431b-b4d7-dc6ee850883e/2023-Primary-Framework-ENG-screen.pdf (accessed 1 Nov. 2023).

Chapter 2. Religious Schools

§1. Introduction

209. The denominational or 'patronage' school system applied in Ireland is firmly supported by (and finds its roots in) Article 42 of the Irish Constitution. Article 42.1 provides:

> The State acknowledges that the primary and natural educator of the child is the Family and guarantees to respect the inalienable right and duty of parents to provide, according to their means, for the religious and moral, intellectual, physical and social education of their children.[422]

210. Defining the role of the State in the provision of education services, Article 42.4 continues that the State is merely obliged to provide 'for' free primary education. It states:

> The State shall provide for free primary education and shall endeavour to supplement and give reasonable aid to private and corporate educational initiative, and, when the public good requires it, provide other educational facilities or institutions with due regard, however, for the rights of parents, especially in the matter of religious and moral formation.

211. As Article 42.4 requires the State to give reasonable aid to private and corporate educational initiatives, the patronage system was also extended to post-primary education.

212. These constitutional provisions have had a major impact on the face of education in Ireland. Of the 3,305 mainstream primary schools recognised by the Department of Education and Skills, over 94% are under the patronage of a named religion.[423] Of the over 700 schools at the post-primary level, approximately 50% are denominational in nature.[424] The vast majority of denominational schools are under the patronage of the Roman Catholic Church, with the 'monopoly enjoyed by

422. Article 42.2 states: 'Parents shall be free to provide this education in their homes or in private schools or in schools recognised or established by the State.' Although 42.3.1° provides 'The State shall not oblige parents in violation of their conscience and lawful preference to send their children to schools established by the State, or to any particular type of school designated by the State', Art. 42.3.2° adds: 'The State shall, however, as guardian of the common good, require in view of actual conditions that the children receive a certain minimum education, moral, intellectual and social.'

423. Darren Lawlor & Shane Burke, *Education in Ireland: Statistical Snapshot* (Houses of the Oireachtas, 2020) available at https://data.oireachtas.ie/ie/oireachtas/libraryResearch/2020/2020-04-03_l-rs-infographic-education-in-ireland-a-statistical-snapshot_en.pdf (accessed 3 Mar. 2021).

424. Darren Lawlor & Shane Burke, Education in Ireland: Statistical Snapshot (Houses of the Oireachtas, 2020) available at https://data.oireachtas.ie/ie/oireachtas/libraryResearch/2020/2020-04-03_l-rs-infographic-education-in-ireland-a-statistical-snapshot_en.pdf (accessed 3 Mar. 2021).

the Catholic Church in education provision'[425] receiving significant attention in both academic and public discourse. According to the 2018–2019 statistical report published by the Department of Education and Skills, 'Catholic schools still comprise the vast majority of primary schools, with 89.4% of schools having a Catholic ethos in 2018.'[426] While the process of divestment is ongoing, the pace has been 'slow'.[427]

213. This encouragement for denominational education has also facilitated the establishment of a number of schools from minority religions in Ireland, with the first Muslim National School benefitting from State funding established in 1990.[428] Nevertheless, notwithstanding the availability of such financial support for the establishment of new schools under the patronage of minority religions, from a practical perspective, such schools will only be established where there is a critical mass of pupils and community engagement supporting the initiative, features which might not always be present, particularly outside of urban areas.[429]

---

425. Claire Hogan, 'The Accommodation of Islam in the Irish Workplace, Classroom and Hospital' in Kathryn O'Sullivan (ed.) *Minority Religions under Irish Law: Islam in National and International Context* 83, 89 (Brill, 2019).
426. Department of Education and Skills, *2018–19 Statistical Report* (2019) 3 available at https://www.education.ie/en/Publications/Statistics/Statistical-Reports/2018-2019-statistical-bulletin.pdf (accessed 28 Aug. 2019).
427. Claire Hogan, 'The Accommodation of Islam in the Irish Workplace, Classroom and Hospital' in Kathryn O'Sullivan (ed.) *Minority Religions under Irish Law: Islam in National and International Context* 83, 90 (Brill, 2019).
428. For more, *see* Tuula Sakaranaho, 'Education and Muslim National Schools in Ireland' in Scharbrodt et al. (eds) *Muslims in Ireland Past and Present* 163 (Edinburgh University Press, 2015).
429. *See* Eoin Daly, *Religion, Law and the Irish State* Ch. 5 (Clarus, 2012). Note s. 10 of the Education Act 1998 (as amended) provides:

    (1) On a request being made for that purpose, the Minister may from time to time designate a school or a proposed school to be a school recognised for the purposes of this Act.
    (2) The Minister may designate a school or a proposed school to be a school recognised for the purposes of this Act where the Minister, on a request being made for that purpose by the patron of a school or a proposed school, is satisfied that:
    (a) the number of students who are attending or are likely to attend the school is such or is likely to be such as to make the school viable;
    (b) in the case of a proposed school, and having regard to the desirability of diversity in the classes of school operating in the area likely to be served by the school, the needs of students attending or likely to attend the school cannot reasonably be met by existing schools;
    (c) the patron undertakes that the school shall provide the curriculum as determined in accordance with s. 30;
    (d) the patron agrees to permit and co-operate with regular inspection and evaluation by the Inspectorate;
    (e) the school complies, or in the case of a proposed school shall comply, with health, safety and building standards as are determined by law and any further such standards as are determined from time to time by the Minister, and
    (f) the patron agrees that the school shall operate in accordance with such regulations as may be made by the Minister from time to time under s. 33 and with this Act and with any other terms and conditions as may reasonably be attached to recognition by the Minister.

§2. Protections for Non-coreligionists

214. Given the dominance of the Roman Catholic Church in the provision of education in Ireland, especially at primary school level, the needs of non-coreligionist pupils have required specific consideration. Section 30(2)(e) of the Education Act 1998 (as amended) provides that in setting the curriculum, the Minister 'shall not require any student to attend instruction in any subject which is contrary to the conscience of the parent of the student or in the case of a student who has reached the age of 18 years, the student'. Thus, the right of withdrawal from religious education classes receives statutory recognition. However, notwithstanding the obvious importance of such a right, questions have been raised as to its sufficiency. The expression of the religious ethos of a school is frequently not confined to formal religious instruction classes but instead 'integrated' or sprinkled across the school's schedule and calendar. In such an environment, the right of withdrawal, though useful, may be of limited practical effect and exposure to the dominant ethos of a school can rarely be avoided. As Barrington J noted in Campaign to *Separate Church and State v. Minister for Education*:

> The Constitution ... distinguishes between religious 'education' and religious 'instruction' – the former being the much wider term. A child who attends a school run by a religious denomination different from his own may have a constitutional right not to attend religious instruction at that school but the Constitution cannot protect him from being influenced, to some degree, by the religious 'ethos' of the school.[430]

215. Despite this, however, he held: 'A religious denomination is not obliged to change the general atmosphere of its school merely to accommodate a child of a different religious persuasion who wishes to attend that school.'[431]

§3. Enrolment Policies

216. Although comprehensive legislation exists to prevent discrimination in the provision of services in Ireland, including on religious grounds,[432] exceptions in the context of education have long generated controversy.[433] Section 7 of the Equal Status Act 2000 (as amended) stated that while there may be no discrimination on the

430. [1998] 3 IR 321 at 357.
431. *Campaign to Separate Church and State v. Minister for Education* [1998] 3 IR 321 at 357. Having regard to the growing Muslim community in Ireland, as Claire Hogan, 'The Accommodation of Islam in the Irish Workplace, Classroom and Hospital' in Kathryn O'Sullivan (ed.) *Minority Religions under Irish Law: Islam in National and International Context* 83, 91 (Brill, 2019) notes, 'a Catholic ethos in schools may not necessarily be inimical to Islam. Indeed, the Catholic Schools Partnership professes a model of inclusion'.
432. *See* Part VII Ch. 7.
433. *See*, for example, Alison Mawhinney, 'Freedom of Religion in the Irish Primary School System: A Failure to Protect Human Rights?' 27(3) *Legal Studies* 379 (2007).

grounds of religion in the provision of goods or services, 'educational establishments', as defined by the legislation, were largely exempted whether or not they were supported by public funds. Pursuant to section 7(2), an educational establishment shall not discriminate in relation to:

(a) the admission or the terms or conditions of admission of a person as a student to the establishment;
(b) the access of a student to any course, facility or benefit provided by the establishment;
(c) any other term or condition of participation in the establishment by a student; Or
(d) the expulsion of a student from the establishment or any other sanction against the student.

217. However, section 7(3)(c) of the Equal Status Act 2000 (as amended) provided that an educational establishment did not discriminate under subsection (2) by reason only that:

> (a) where the establishment is not a third-level institution and admits students of one gender only, it refuses to admit as a student a person who is not of that gender,
> (b) where the establishment is an institution established for the purpose of providing training to ministers of religion and admits students of only one gender or religious belief, it refuses to admit as a student a person who is not of that gender or religious belief,
> (c) where the establishment is a school providing primary or post-primary education to students and the objective of the school is to provide education in an environment which promotes certain religious values, it admits persons of a particular religious denomination in preference to others or it refuses to admit as a student a person who is not of that denomination and, in the case of a refusal, it is proved that the refusal is essential to maintain the ethos of the school … .

218. Thus, it was not discrimination where a school providing primary or post-primary education to students preferred persons of a particular religious denomination over others where the objective of the school was to provide a denominational education. Consequently, where it was proved that a refusal was essential to maintain the ethos of a school, such a school could refuse to admit a student who was not of that denomination. The constitutionality of the section – and the so-called baptism barrier – was confirmed in the Irish courts and was regarded as an important aspect of the protection afforded to religious freedom in Ireland.[434]

434. *See In the matter of Article 26 of the Constitution and in the matter of The Equal Status Bill, 1997* [1997] 2 IR 388. The Bill was referred by the President of Ireland to the Supreme Court under Art. 26 of the Constitution to test its constitutionality. While other provisions of the Bill were found to

219. Despite this, the section continued to generate controversy. As Mawhinney observed:

> Through providing exemptions from equality legislation to religious organisations, in a situation where these bodies are in a near-monopolistic position, the Irish State is disregarding its responsibility to protect the right to nondiscrimination, the right to education and the right to freedom of religion of those who do not adhere to the ethos of these religious service providers. While the permitted discrimination may be deemed to have a legitimate aim, the means of achieving that aim cannot be considered reasonable and proportionate in a context where the outcome may be mean that minority belief child has no school to go to or that a parent feels pressurised to conform to a particular religion through the baptism of a child.[435]

220. The exception has, however, recently been abolished for the majority of schools pursuant to the Education (Admissions to Schools) Act 2018.[436] Consequently, primary schools generally may no longer use religion as a basis for admission and may not prioritise students based on their religious beliefs. However, limited exceptions exist. For example, minority religion schools continue to receive heightened protection and may continue to give priority to a student of that religion who is seeking admission to the school. Seeking to ensure transparency and fairness, the Act moreover requires all schools to publish their admissions policies, which will include particulars of their provisions for pupils who decline to participate in religious instruction.

---

be unconstitutional, s. 7(3)(c) was not considered and thus not impugned. It is believed that the constitutionality of the section was accepted in light of an earlier decision whereby analogous provisions in the context of employment policies were upheld as constitutional, *see In the Matter of Article 26 and in the Matter of the Employment Equality Bill, 1996* [1997] 2 IR 321. *See* Gerard Hogan & Gerry Whyte, *JM Kelly: The Irish Constitution* 2017 (Butterworths, 2003). *See also McGrath and Ó Ruairc v. Trustees of Maynooth College* [1979] ILRM 166.

435. Alison Mawhinney, 'A Discriminating Education System: Religious Admission Policies in Irish Schools and International Human Rights Law' 20(4) *International Journal of Children's Rights* 603 (2012). She added 'International human rights bodies have consistently highlighted the incompatibility of Irish religious admissions policies with international human rights standards.' In particular, as the Irish Human Rights and Equality Commission highlighted, the exemption in the Equal Status Act for religious schools was 'assessed four times in recent years against human rights standards that are provided for in global human rights treaties that the State has agreed to be bound by', *see* the Irish Human Rights and Equality Commission, *Observation on Education (Admission to Schools) Bill 2016* (2016) 8–11 available at https://www.ihrec.ie/app/uploads/2016/11/Observations-on-Education-Admission-to-Schools-Bill-2016.pdf (accessed 22 Aug. 2017). These are: the International Convention on the Elimination of All forms of Racial Discrimination, which Ireland ratified in 2000; the International Covenant on Civil and Political Rights, which Ireland ratified in 1989; the International Covenant on Economic, Social and Cultural Rights, which Ireland ratified in 1989; and the UN Convention on the Rights of the Child, which Ireland ratified in 1992.

436. *See* https://www.education.ie/en/Press-Events/Press-Releases/2018-press-releases/PR18-10-03.html (accessed 18 Jan. 2021).

Part X. Matrimonial and Family Law

Introduction

221. As Connolly observes, the family has 'occupied a core position in public debates about the "common good" and national identity formation in Ireland since the foundation of the State'.[437] In particular, the marital family continues to dominate Irish family structures and receives privileged mention and protection in the Irish Constitution. As the Supreme Court noted in 2017: 'Despite the factual reality that many couples do not choose to marry, marriage remains a central feature of Irish life for the majority.'[438] However, notwithstanding the former dominance of the Roman Catholic Church in the jurisdiction, developments, particularly at a constitutional level, 'have resulted in a legal institution of marriage that cannot be described in terms of traditional Christian doctrine'.[439] Among these key developments were the introduction of no-fault divorce in 1996 and, in particular, the amendment of the Constitution providing for the introduction of same-sex marriage in 2015. This part will consider these developments and will place particular attention on recent reforms in relation to the formalities required for entry into a legally recognised marriage in Ireland pursuant to the Civil Registration Act 2004 (as amended). It will also have regard to the recognition of foreign marriage and divorce before turning to address the legal position of religious family law.

437. Linda Connolly, 'Locating the Irish Family' in Linda Connolly (ed.) *The 'Irish' Family* 10 (Routledge, 2015).
438. *HAH v. SAA & ors* [2017] IESC 40 at [99].
439. *HAH v. SAA & ors* [2017] IESC 40 at [98].

Chapter 1. Legal Position of Religious Marriage

§1. CONSTITUTIONAL PROTECTION FOR MARRIAGE

222. The legal importance of the institution of marriage is heightened in an Irish context, given the protection afforded to the marital family under the Irish Constitution. From a constitutional perspective, it is the marital family, specifically, which enjoys an exalted position. Article 41.1.1° states:

> The State recognises the Family as the natural primary and fundamental unit group of Society, and as a moral institution possessing inalienable and imprescriptible rights, antecedent and superior to all positive law.

223. Moreover, Article 41.3.1° explicitly states, 'The State pledges itself to guard with special care the institution of Marriage, on which the Family is founded, and to protect it against attack.'[440] Given this recognition, the ability (or otherwise) to access marriage has received considerable legislative attention, with numerous amendments introduced in recent decades reforming how parties may marry[441] and who may marry whom.[442]

§2. MARRIAGE FORMALITIES UNDER IRISH LAW

224. Prior to the modernisation of the formalities for entry into marriage in Ireland, Irish wedding law was notoriously complex, with the governing law dating from the nineteenth century.[443] Depending on the form of wedding, whether civil or religious, there were different requirements to be met. In relation to religious weddings, in particular, the rules were especially complicated.[444] Certain privileges relating to the solemnisation and wedding venue were granted to some religious groups and not others, while the system of preliminaries applied to weddings also

---

440. Note, in March 2024, a referendum will be held on the 39th Amendment to the Constitution. It proposes to amend both Art. 41.1.1 and Art. 41.3.1, removing the constitutional preference for marriage and instead recognizing the family 'whether founded on marriage or on other durable relationships'.
441. The Civil Registration Act 2004 (as amended) liberalised the formalities for entry into a legally recognised marriage, as discussed below. *See also* Susan Leahy & Kathryn O'Sullivan, 'Changing Conceptions of Marriage in Ireland: Law and Practice' 30(3) *Child and Family Law Quarterly* 279–300 (2018); Deirdre McGowan, 'Governed by Marriage Law' 25(3) *Social and Legal Studies* 311 (2016).
442. *See* Part VII Ch. 2 above.
443. Note, in particular, the Marriages (Ireland) Act 1844 as amended by the Registration of Marriages (Ireland) Act 1863.
444. In the Irish context, they centred largely upon marriages performed according to the rites of the Roman Catholic Church.

developed in an ad hoc manner.[445] Although reforming efforts were undertaken in 1995, these initiatives merely served to further compound the difficulties.[446]

225. Reflecting on these challenges, the Minister for Social and Family Affairs noted in 2004:

> The law in relation to marriage is complex, uneven and not easily understood by the public or by those involved in administration. Procedures are set down in law for the solemnisation of marriage by registrars and some religious bodies. However, there are other churches which are not adequately catered for by current legislation. There is a need to provide a universal framework that recognises and underpins marriage as a solemn contract, streamlines procedures, provides clarity and formalities to be observed and retains the safeguards and strengths of the current system.[447]

226. In this context, and as part of a wider reform of the civil registration system applied in Ireland, marriage law reform, seeking to introduce standard rules and procedures for the solemnisation of all weddings and aiming to 'ensure that the important legal significance and obligations of marriage are clearly understood by the couple, the witnesses and by society in general' became the focus of legislative attention.[448]

227. Today, the Civil Registration Act 2004 (as amended) confers legal recognition on three types of wedding ceremonies.[449] The first option is a civil wedding conducted by a civil registrar who is employed by the Health Service Executive. The second option is a religious wedding ceremony and the final option, available

445. The rules and procedures regarding venues for marriages were directly related to the type of licences for marriage available while the location for Roman Catholic ceremonies was not regulated by statute. The legal requirements for Roman Catholic marriage ceremonies, the most common ceremonies conducted in Ireland, were still governed by common law.

446. *See* Susan Leahy & Kathryn O'Sullivan, 'Changing Conceptions of Marriage in Ireland: Law and Practice' 30(3) *Child and Family Law Quarterly* 279 (2018).

447. Civil Registration Bill 2003: Committee Stage (Resumed), *Select Committee on Social and Family Affairs* (4 Feb. 2004) per Minister Mary Coughlan. She also noted: 'There is currently a very complex, uneven system in place in regard to an intended marriage which involves obtaining various forms of licences and certificates before a marriage can take place. This has led to confusion among the public and the solemnisers.'

448. Civil Registration Bill 2003: Committee Stage (Resumed), *Select Committee on Social and Family Affairs* (4 Feb. 2004) per Minister Mary Coughlan. Meanwhile, notwithstanding the powerful constitutional protection for the institution of marriage and the continuing pro-marriage orientation of governmental policy, Deirdre McGowan, *The Normalising Power of Marriage Law: An Irish Genealogy 1945 – 2010* 319 (PhD, Maynooth University, 2015) also noted the 'growing consensus' which emerged in the late 1990s and the early 2000s on the need to reform marriage law: 'As new forms of stable [unmarried] partnership became visible, and demanded the advantages conferred on married couples, human rights and equality arguments were deployed to re-enforce the privileges of long-term conjugality.' *See* below for more.

449. *See* General Introduction, §2 above for the latest statistics on the types of wedding ceremonies celebrated in Ireland.

since 2012, is a secular wedding ceremony.[450] Significantly, from the point of view of simplicity and marking a welcome development on the previously complicated legal provisions, the preliminaries for marriage are the same regardless of what form of ceremony is anticipated. The requirements for solemnisation are also largely similar, apart from requirements regarding the location, which may differ depending on the form of ceremony which is being contemplated.

228. To contract a legally valid marriage in Ireland, intending spouses must provide written notice of their intention to marry not less than three months prior to the date on which the marriage is to be solemnised;[451] they must present themselves at the registrar's office not less than five days before the date of the wedding; and they must declare in the presence of the registrar that there is no impediment to the marriage as per section 46(1).[452] They must also be over 18 years of age.[453] An MRF must be completed, and a marriage cannot be solemnised unless the parties present the MRF to the individual who will solemnise the marriage for examination as required under section 48. The MRF must be signed by the parties to the marriage after the ceremony and returned to the registrar for formal registration of the marriage.

229. Regarding the ceremony itself, the requirements under Irish law are not unduly onerous. With regard to the venue requirement, the 2004 Act has greatly simplified the process.[454] Today, there is no concept of a registered venue for wedding ceremonies in Ireland. The fundamental requirement is that to be suitable for a wedding ceremony, a venue must be a 'place that is open to the public'.[455] Beyond this requirement, religious and secular solemnisers are free to choose the venues in

450. Having regard to the Civil Registration (Amendment) Bill 2012 which sought to facilitate secular ceremonies, Minister Mary Coughlan noted: 'This legislation is a small but significant piece of the mosaic in the development of social and personal freedoms in Ireland, the cornerstone of which is respect. We should respect people from different traditions and backgrounds and their ethical and moral frameworks. We should use the Oireachtas as the appropriate place in which to legislate to reflect all of the different religious, ethical and humanist frameworks in Ireland.' *See* Civil Registration (Amendment) Bill 2012: Second and Subsequent Stages, *Seanad Eireann* (6 Dec. 2012). *See* below for more.

451. However, *see* s. 47 for exceptions.

452. Irish law, for example, does not permit bigamy or polygamy. Pursuant to s. 2(2) of the Civil Registration Act 2004, there is an impediment to a marriage if one or both of the parties are already married.

453. In relation to the age requirement, it was possible for individuals aged 16 or 17 to marry with a court exemption. However, s. 45 of the Domestic Violence Act 2018 now abolishes such exemptions.

454. Prior to the commencement of the 2004 Act (as amended), the rules regarding venue were not universally applicable to all denominations. Moreover, for civil marriages, a registrar could only conduct a wedding in his or her office. This greatly restricted the options for persons wishing to get married in a civil ceremony. It was noted: 'The restriction on civil marriage to the registrar's office gives rise to a considerable number of complaints regarding capacity … location and environment.' Civil Registration Bill 2003: Committee Stage (Resumed), *Select Committee on Social and Family Affairs* (4 Feb. 2004) per Minister Mary Coughlan.

455. Section 51(2A). Outdoor ceremonies in grounds lying 'near to' and 'usually enjoyed with' the public building are also recognised.

which ceremonies will be conducted.[456] Regarding civil marriages, while civil registrars are permitted to conduct weddings outside of their offices, the rules on the venues they can use are a little more strict, requiring that a venue must be pre-approved.[457] Pursuant to section 51(2)(c) of the 2004 Act (as amended), an exception to the location requirements can be made where one or both of the couple is seriously ill, and a doctor has certified that they are unable by reason of their illness to attend at a place that is open to the public. In such instances, the local Superintendent Registrar (or the Registrar General) may grant approval for the wedding to take place at a venue that is not open to the public.

230. While the regulations regarding the location of a wedding ceremony have been relaxed, the focus of regulation has instead been placed on the solemniser.[458] Central to compliance with the formalities set down in the 2004 Act (as amended) is that the marriage must be solemnised by a registered solemniser pursuant to section 51: namely, a nominated member of a religious body whose name is included on the Register of Solemnisers or who has secured temporary authorisation to solemnise a religious marriage under section 57. Criminal sanctions are set down for scenarios where a person who is not a registered solemniser or holder of temporary authorisation conducts a wedding ceremony in such a way as to lead the parties to the marriage to believe that he or she is solemnising a valid marriage.[459] Criminal sanctions are also included for situations where a registered solemniser does not adhere to the formalities set down in the 2004 Act (as amended), for example, in solemnising a marriage without an MRF having been given to him/her before the solemnisation for examination.[460]

231. As alluded to above, the Civil Registration (Amendment) Act 2012 extended the categories of bodies and organisations that may apply to the Registrar General for the registration of their members to solemnise marriages.[461] Although prior to the amendment, only the Health Services Executive and religious bodies[462]

---

456. This 'public place' requirement is liable to create difficulties for the legal recognition of Islamic *nikah* ceremonies where such ceremonies may take place in a private house, *see* Kathryn O'Sullivan, 'Religious-Only Marriages & Officiant-Based Marriage Law Reform: An Irish Perspective' 49 *Family Law* 1156 (2019). *See also* Kathryn O'Sullivan, 'Location, Location, Location: The Future of Weddings Law in Ireland and England' 43(3) *Journal of Social Welfare and Family Law* (2021) 307–326.
457. Note, despite the fact that the liberalisation of the rules relating to venues has introduced a relatively straightforward framework, some uncertainties have arisen, *see* Susan Leahy & Kathryn O'Sullivan, 'Changing Conceptions of Marriage in Ireland: Law and Practice' 30(3) *Child and Family Law Quarterly* 279 (2018).
458. In this regard, the Irish approach of adopting a so-called system of wedding regulation mirrors that applied under the Marriage (Scotland) Act 1977. For analysis, *see* Kathryn O'Sullivan, 'Religious-Only Marriages & Officiant-Based Marriage Law Reform: An Irish Perspective' 49 *Family Law* 1156 (2019).
459. Section 69(10)(b) of the 2004 Act (as amended) discussed above in Part VII Ch. 8.
460. Section 69(10)(c) of the 2004 Act (as amended) discussed above in Part VII Ch. 8.
461. The Civil Registration (Amendment) Act 2012 became law on 23 Jan. 2013.
462. Per s. 45 of the 2004 Act (as amended), 'religious body' means an organised group of people members of which meet regularly for common religious worship.

could apply for registration in the Register of Solemnisers, this was extended to permit members of secular bodies to conduct legally recognised weddings. Section 45A(1) of the Civil Registration Act 2004, as inserted by section 3 of the Civil Registration (Amendment) Act 2012, provides a definition of a 'secular body':

> (1) For the purposes of this Part, a body shall … be a secular body if it is an organised group of people and–
> (a) it has not fewer than 50 members,
> (b) its principal objects are secular, ethical and humanist,
> (c) members of the body meet regularly in relation to their beliefs and in furtherance of the objects referred to in paragraph (b),
> (d) it does not have any rules regarding marriage or the solemnisation of marriages that contravene the requirements of this Act or any other enactment or rule of law,
> (e) it is shown to the satisfaction of an tArd-Chláraitheoir to be a body that has appropriate procedures in writing for selecting, training and accrediting members as fit and proper persons to solemnise marriages,
> (f) it is a body that, on the date of its making of an application under section 54 or 57, has been in existence for a continuous period of not less than 5 years,
> (g) it is a body–
> (i) that is entitled to an exemption under section 207 or 208 of the Taxes Consolidation Act 1997, and was so entitled for a continuous period of not less than five years immediately preceding the date of the body's most recent application under section 54 or 57, and
> (ii) in respect of which–
> (I) a number (commonly referred to as a CHY [Charity] number) stands issued by the Revenue Commissioners for the purposes of that exemption, and
> (II) that number stood issued for a continuous period of not less than 5 years immediately preceding the date of its most recent application under section 54 or 57,
> (h) it is a body that does not have the making of profit as one of its principal objects, and
> (i) it maintains a register of its members.

232. Section 45A(2) moreover outlines bodies or organisations that will not be considered a 'secular body' for the purposes of the part. These include: a political party, or a body that promotes a political party or candidate; a body that promotes a political cause; or a body that promotes purposes that are:

(i) unlawful;
(ii) contrary to public morality;
(iii) contrary to public policy;

(iv) in support of terrorism or terrorist activities, whether in the State or outside the State; or
(v) for the benefit of an organisation membership of which is unlawful.

233. Thus, in order to solemnise a marriage pursuant to the Civil Registration Act, a secular body must be ethical and humanist and must not promote a political cause.[463] Until very recently, only one secular body had received this authorisation, namely, the Humanist Association of Ireland. As a result, almost all secular wedding ceremonies conducted since April 2013 were humanist ceremonies. According to the latest Registrar of Solemnisers,[464] there are more than forty secular solemnisers representing the Humanist Association of Ireland. The only other secular body with a registered solemniser is Aisling Árann Teoranta which was added in April 2015.[465] Organisations such as Atheist Ireland, which actively promote the political cause of separation of Church and State, do not qualify under the Act.

234. Notwithstanding that non-compliance with marriage formalities would normally be expected to render a marriage void,[466] the application of this rule in the context of Irish marriage law has raised some doubts. Some commentators have suggested that while non-compliance with age or notice requirements will render a marriage void (unless the relevant exemptions have been obtained from the courts), '[t]he general principle outside these requirements is that the non-observance of or a defect in any of the other prescribed formalities does not invalidate a marriage unless both parties were aware of it at the time of the ceremony'.[467] Although this precedent may continue to apply to the formalities introduced by the 2004 Act, it has recently been pointed out that it is not safe to assume so.[468] The so-called knowledge rule emerged from the 1985 decision of *IE v. WE*,[469] wherein it was held that to invalidate a marriage for non-compliance with formalities, it was 'necessary to establish not only that there should have been a conscious disregard of [the formalities] but also that both parties to the apparent marriage should have been aware of the defect'.[470] This rule was subsequently approved in *DC v. NM* (falsely known as NC).[471] However, this precedent predates the introduction of the 2004 legislation and may no longer be authoritative. Equally, although the former regime appeared

463. No such restrictions apply to religious bodies.
464. *See*, https://www.gov.ie/en/publication/077ce8-register-of-solemnisers/ (accessed 1 Nov. 2023). Note, the report was last refreshed 1 Oct. 2023.
465. Dara Ó Maoildhia who appears to run this body is a self-described Celtic priest, *see* http://www.daramolloy.com/index.html (accessed 24 Jul. 2019).
466. If this was the case, the parties to this void marriage would not be entitled to ancillary relief such as maintenance or property division under the Family Law Acts 1995 and 1996, *see* Susan Leahy & Kathryn O'Sullivan, 'Recognition of Muslim Marriages Ceremonies in Ireland: An Analysis' in Kathryn O'Sullivan (ed.) *Minority Religions under Irish Law: Islam in National and International Context* 108–130 (Brill, 2019).
467. Louise Crowley, *Family Law* 58 (Round Hall, 2013).
468. Susan Leahy & Kathryn O'Sullivan, 'Changing Conceptions of Marriage in Ireland: Law and Practice' 30(3) *Child and Family Law Quarterly* 279 (2018).
469. [1985] ILRM 691.
470. *IE v. WE* [1985] ILRM 691, 695.
471. [1997] 2 IR 218.

to draw a distinction between the age and notice requirements (described as 'substantive requirements for marriage') and other formalities, section 51(5) provides that the requirements for marriage ceremonies set out above (i.e., that the ceremony be performed by a registered solemniser, with both parties and witnesses present, in a public venue, where the relevant declarations are made) are also 'substantive'. In the absence of definitive clarification as to the effects of non-compliance with the formalities, it remains impossible to predict precisely when non-compliance with formalities will render a marriage void.

235. While clarification of the law in relation to non-compliance with the formalities remains awaited, calls for the development and reform of other aspects of Irish marriage law continue to draw attention. In particular, the focus has been placed on the need for the reform of the degrees of relationship based on consanguinity or affinity, which prevent persons from marrying each other in the jurisdiction, as noted above in Part VII Chapter 2, albeit no reform has been forthcoming. Calls for the reform of the law relating to bigamy have also been advanced.[472] However, progress has been made in responding to the perceived threat of purported 'marriages of convenience' or 'sham marriages' with recent amendments to the regime paving the way for the increased involvement of the criminal justice system in an area which traditionally has been almost entirely the preserve of civil rules. Pursuant to the Civil Registration (Amendment) Act 2014, registrars are empowered to object to marriages which they believe are marriages of convenience, defined as:

> a marriage where at least one of the parties to the marriage (a) at the time of the marriage is a foreign national, and (b) enters into the marriage solely for the purpose of securing an immigration advantage for at least one of the parties to the marriage.[473]

236. Moreover, pursuant to section 38(1) of the Domestic Violence Act 2018, Irish law now recognises an offence of forced marriage. It provides that a person commits an offence where s/he engages in 'relevant conduct' for the purpose of causing another person to enter into a 'ceremony of marriage'.[474] 'Relevant conduct' refers to violence, threats, undue influence or any form of coercion or duress.[475] The new legislation also protects against the threat of an adult or a child being removed or lured from Ireland to another territory and forced to enter into a marriage under section 38(2).

472. Susan Leahy, 'Criminal Offences Relating to Marriage Formation: Reflections on Recent Developments' 22(4) *Irish Journal of Family Law* 87 (2019).

473. *See* s. 2 of the Civil Registration Act 2004 (as amended) as inserted by s. 3 of the Civil Registration (Amendment) Act 2014. *See also* Susan Leahy, 'Criminal Offences Relating to Marriage Formation: Reflections on Recent Developments' 22(4) *Irish Journal of Family Law* 87 (2019).

474. Under s. 38(11), 'ceremony of marriage' means any religious, civil or secular ceremony of marriage, whether legally binding or not.

475. Section 38(11). Note, the penalty on summary conviction is a class A fine or a term of imprisonment up to twelve months or both. The penalty on conviction on indictment is a fine or a maximum term of imprisonment of seven years, or both. *see* Susan Leahy, 'Criminal Offences Relating to

§3. COHABITATION LEGISLATION

237. Notwithstanding that the 2004 Act (as amended) reformed and modernised the formalities required for entry into a legally recognised marriage in Ireland, the early 2000s also saw increased momentum for the recognition of other marriage-like relationships in the jurisdiction. Although pre-marital cohabitation was socially and culturally frowned upon for most of the twentieth century – and '[p]regnancy outside marriage in Ireland was utterly taboo'[476] – changes, particularly through the 1980s and 1990s, saw a significant shift in social and cultural mores. As more and more couples chose to cohabit, increasing pressure came on the Irish Government to react with appropriate legislative initiatives to reflect this new family form.[477]

238. Responding to highly effective rights-based and equality-based campaigning and seeking to ensure the law was 'humane, tolerant and protective',[478] the Irish Government enacted the Civil Partnership and Certain Rights and Obligations of Cohabitants Act 2010. A 'cohabitant' for the purposes of the Act is defined by section 172 as 'one of 2 adults (whether of the same or the opposite sex) who live together as a couple in an intimate and committed relationship and who are not related to each other within the prohibited degrees of relationship or married to each other or civil partners of each other'.[479] Where a cohabiting relationship breaks down, 'qualified cohabitants' may seek financial provision in the form of maintenance, pension adjustment orders or property adjustment orders.[480] 'Qualified cohabitants' are defined as those who have lived together for five years or, where

Marriage Formation: Reflections on Recent Developments' 22(4) *Irish Journal of Family Law* 87, 91 (2019) argues more needs to be done, however.

476. Linda Connolly, 'Locating the Irish Family' in Linda Connolly (ed.) *The 'Irish' Family* 28 (Routledge, 2015).

477. Note, while cohabitation continues to be popular, it is usually a precursor to marriage. The report on 'Households and Families' taken from the results of the 2016 census notes that '[a]s cohabitation is often a precursor to marriage in Ireland, these couples tend to be younger on average than married couples': Central Statistics Office, *Census of Population 2016: Profile 4 Households and Families* (2017). Margaret Fine-Davis, *Attitudes to Family Formation in Ireland: Findings from the Nationwide Study* (Family Support Agency, 2011) also found that 'cohabitation is widely accepted and seen as a step in progression towards marriage'.

478. Civil Partnership and Certain Rights and Obligations of Cohabitants Bill 2009: Second Stage, *Seanad Éireann* debate (7 Jul. 2010) per then Minister for Equality and Law Reform Dermot Ahern.

479. Section 172(2) states: 'In determining whether or not 2 adults are cohabitants, the court shall take into account all the circumstances of the relationship and in particular shall have regard to the following:

(a) the duration of the relationship;
(b) the basis on which the couple live together;
(c) the degree of financial dependence of either adult on the other and any agreements in respect of their finances;
(d) the degree and nature of any financial arrangements between the adults including any joint purchase of an estate or interest in land or joint acquisition of personal property;
(e) whether there are one or more dependent children;
(f) whether one of the adults cares for and supports the children of the other; and
(g) the degree to which the adults present themselves to others as a couple.'

480. Note, pursuant to s. 194, orders for provision from the estate of a deceased cohabitant may also be sought.

there are dependent children, for two years.[481] Moreover, they must prove that they are financially dependent as a result of the relationship or the ending of it if they are to seek relief.[482] Notwithstanding that the legislation represents an important addition to the Statute Book, however, recent research has cast some doubt on the extent to which it actually provides meaningful protection to financially weaker parties on relationship breakdown, with the challenges in accessing the regime being ever more apparent.[483] Whether or to what extent the outcome of the referendum on the 39th Amendment to the Constutition (due to be held in March 2024 and seeking to recognise not just marital families but also those founded on other 'durable relationships') will result in the review or reform of the legislative scheme, remains to be seen.[484]

§4. Civil Partnership and Same-Sex Marriage

239. The Civil Partnership and Certain Rights and Obligations of Cohabitants Act 2010 also introduced civil partnership for same-sex couple relationships. Although civil partnership largely mirrored marriage, subtle distinctions were drawn, with 'some inelegant attempts to differentiate it for the purposes of constitutional compliance' observed.[485] However, while the 2010 Act represented an important step forward for gay rights campaigners, calls for marriage equality continued to gain pace. Wary of any political fall-out, the issue was sent by the Irish Government to a reform-oriented body composed primarily of ordinary Irish citizens, the 'Constitutional Convention'.[486] Following the recommendation of the Convention, a referendum was held to decide the matter in May 2015. With a 60% turnout delivering a 62% 'yes' vote, the marriage equality referendum was passed. Giving effect to the result, Article 41.4 of the Irish Constitution now provides that

---

481. Section 172(5). Section 172(2) provides a list of considerations which a judge must take into account when determining whether the parties are 'qualified cohabitants'.
482. Section 173.
483. *See* Kathryn O'Sullivan, 'Cohabitant Protection on Relationship Breakdown in Ireland: A Lesson in Illusory Justice?' (2023) *International Journal of Law, Policy & the Family* (forthcoming in print) available online at, https://academic.oup.com/lawfam/article/37/1/ebad017/7225500 (accessed 1 Nov. 2023).
484. If the referendum passes, it will likely result in pressue for the liberalization of the scheme applied under Part 15 of the 2010 Act. However, even if the referendum fails to pass, there may be renewed interest in at least reviewing the scheme to determine its effectiveness in protecting potentially vulnerable financially weaker cohabitants on relationship breakdown.
485. Deirdre McGowan, *The Normalising Power of Marriage Law: An Irish Genealogy 1945 – 2010,* 323 (PhD, Maynooth University, 2015). The then Minster for Justice, Equality and Law Reform Dermot Ahern noted, 'While there is the need to respect the entitlement to equality that same-sex partners enjoy under Article 40.1 of the Constitution, there is also the need to respect the special protection which Article 41 gives to marriage.' Civil Partnership Bill 2009: Second Stage, *Dáil Éireann* debate (3 Dec. 2009).
486. *See* Brian Tobin, 'Marriage Equality in Ireland: The Politico-Legal Context' 30(2) *International Journal of Law, Policy and the Family* 115 (2016).

'marriage may be contracted in accordance with law by two parties without distinction as to their sex'.[487] At a legislative level, the Marriage Act 2015 was also introduced, and the ability of same-sex couples to apply for civil partnership under the 2010 Act was removed.

§5. Divorce under Irish Law

240. Reflecting the dominance of Catholic social teaching at the legislative and political level in the first half of the twentieth century, a ban on divorce was introduced by the Second Constitution of Ireland, published in 1937.[488] As a result, where a marriage broke down, spouses had two possible options. First, they could choose to enter into a separation agreement which constituted a private arrangement. Second, they could try to avail of a divorce a mensa et thoro. It, however, was only available on the grounds of adultery, cruelty or unnatural practices and did not affect the dissolution of a marriage or allow the parties to remarry. Spousal support, moreover, represented the only ancillary relief open to the Court. In 1986, an attempt to remove the ban through a referendum on the Tenth Amendment to the Constitution Bill 1986 was rejected by almost two-thirds of the population. Although progress in legislating for marital breakdown was made with the Judicial Separation and Family Law Reform Act 1989 – which established the grounds for the award of a decree of judicial separation and empowered the court for the first time to make a wide range of ancillary relief orders including property adjustment orders – the need for a remedy of divorce remained. Although 37,245 'separated' individuals were recorded in the 1986 census,[489] this number had risen by almost 50% to 55,143 persons by 1991.[490] Adopting the 'comprehensive proposals' of the White Paper on Marital Breakdown in September 1992,[491] the Government held a second referendum on divorce in 1995 and adopted a more proactive approach in campaigning for a 'yes' vote. On this occasion, the referendum passed with a majority of just 9,114 votes and the support of 50.28% of the electorate.[492] The Family Law (Divorce) Act 1996 (as amended) subsequently came into effect on 27 February 1997, which supplemented the new constitutional provision and empowered the judiciary to order a decree of divorce.

---

487. Note also, the Gender Recognition Act 2015 allows an individual to have his/her chosen gender legally recognised on their birth certificate. Such birth certificates can be used for marriage formalities, allowing the individual to be recognised as her chosen gender for marriage solemnisation.
488. Such a ban did not form part of the First Constitution of the Irish Free State in 1922.
489. Central Statistics Office, *Census 86: Summary Population Report* (Stationery Office, 1987).
490. Central Statistics Office, *Census 91: Summary Population Report* (Stationery Office, 1993). Consequently, the volume of deserted wives receiving social welfare payments had more than trebled, *see* Department of Social Welfare, *Statistical Information on Social Welfare Services 1991* (PL 8806, 1992). *See also* Peter Ward, 'The Path to Divorce' 12 *Irish Law Times* 29 (1994).
491. Peter Ward, 'The Path to Divorce' 12 *Irish Law Times* 29 (1994).
492. For discussion of the historical context for the introduction of divorce, *see* Kathryn O'Sullivan, 'The Legacy Continues: Ancillary Relief on Divorce in Ireland' 25(3) *Journal of Family Studies* 337 (2019).

241. Although the period between when a couple separated and when they could proceed to seek a divorce was originally set in the Constitution as a minimum of four years,[493] this has been significantly reduced. In May 2019, a referendum on the criteria for divorce – the Thirty-Eighth Amendment to the Constitution – was held. The referendum proposed leaving the wait period required for a divorce to be set by the legislature. Reflecting the changing social climate, the referendum was overwhelmingly passed by 82.1% of the electorate.[494]

242. As a result of these updates, Article 41.3.2° of the Irish Constitution now provides:

> A Court designated by law may grant a dissolution of marriage where, but only where, it is satisfied that
>
> i. there is no reasonable prospect of a reconciliation between the spouses;
> ii. such provision as the Court considers proper having regard to the circumstances exists or will be made for the spouses, any children of either or both of them and any other person prescribed by law; and
> iii. any further conditions prescribed by law are complied with.[495]

243. Section 5(1) of the Family Law (Divorce) Act 1996 (as amended) further provides that in seeking a divorce, the spouses must have 'lived apart from one another for a period of, or periods amounting to, at least two years during the previous three years'.

244. Notwithstanding the significant social shifts and the growing acceptability of divorce in the jurisdiction, marital separation as a social phenomenon has remained low by European standards.[496] As Connolly explains, 'Ireland has maintained one of the lowest divorce rates in Europe. Change in the legal situation did not stimulate a rapid increase in divorce.'[497] Moreover, as Fahy notes, serial family

---

493. Couples were originally required to be living separate and apart for a period of four of the previous five years.
494. *See*, for example, Jack Horgan-Jones, 'Divorce Referendum to Reduce Required Wait Period Passes by Huge Margin' *Irish Times*, 25 May 2019.
495. Note also, a divorce under religious law, for example, a canonical annulment, does not have direct civil effect. Where a party obtains a religious divorce or annulment only and subsequently remarries civilly, they will be committing the offence of bigamy. As Louise Crowley, *Family Law* 721 (Roundhall, 2013) explains: 'there is no right to remarry if a canonical annulment only has been secured, and in the absence of a judicial decree of nullity'. For discussion of the law of nullity in Ireland (and the need for reform), *see* 722–726.
496. Linda Connolly, 'Locating the Irish Family' in Linda Connolly (ed.) *The 'Irish' Family* 24 (Routledge, 2015).
497. Linda Connolly, 'Locating the Irish Family' in Linda Connolly (ed.) *The 'Irish' Family* 24 (Routledge, 2015).

formation is 'still relatively unusual' in Ireland,[498] and low interest in second marriage has been observed.[499] It has been noted:

> Traditional forms of family life (such as the life-long, nuclear family based on heterosexual marriage and an unequal gender-based division of labour in the home) continue and are sustained alongside new family forms emerging in contemporary Ireland, suggesting that in reality a complex tension exists between tradition, modernity and postmodernity.[500]

§6. Foreign Marriage and Divorce Recognition

245. The importance of private international law has steadily been increasing in Ireland in recent times, particularly in the context of foreign marriage and divorce recognition. Pursuant to the principle of lex loci celebrationis, Irish law recognises marriages contracted in a foreign country that comply with the laws of that country unless they conflict with fundamental requirements regarding validity.[501] Where issues have arisen in the absence of well-developed legislation governing the recognition of foreign marriages, they have been determined by the courts.

246. Questions regarding the status of actually or potentially polygamous marriages performed outside of Ireland have long proved problematic. Until very recent times, the position was held that, as a general rule, neither actually nor potentially polygamous marriages were capable of being recognised under Irish law but were instead viewed as being contrary to public policy.[502] The recent decision of the Supreme Court in *HAH v. SAA* & ors has seen a shift in policy in this regard, however.[503] The Supreme Court confirmed that a potentially polygamous marriage is capable of being recognised as legally valid in Ireland and may be recognised as of the date of inception.[504] Justice O'Malley, speaking for the Court, noted:

---

498. Tony Fahey, 'The Family in Ireland in the New Millennium' in Linda Connolly (ed.) *The 'Irish' Family* 57 (Routledge, 2015).
499. Tony Fahey, 'The Family in Ireland in the New Millennium' in Linda Connolly (ed.) *The 'Irish' Family* 65 (Routledge, 2015).
500. Linda Connolly, 'Locating the Irish Family' in Linda Connolly (ed.) *The 'Irish' Family* 34 (Routledge, 2015). Similarly, Tony Fahey, 'The Family in Ireland in the New Millennium' in Linda Connolly (ed.) *The 'Irish' Family* 67–68 (Routledge, 2015) notes: 'There is a new consensus on norms of family behaviour, much of which would have been counted as shocking a generation ago. However, the manner in which people live out these norms in their daily lives is a complex matter and leads to results that are not always different from the past as the level of normative change would lead one to expect: the stable nuclear family is still the dominant model in practice, and deviations from that model often have as much to do with social disadvantage as with free choice and alternative life-styles.'
501. For example, public policy requirements in Irish law including the capacity to marry.
502. *See* Máire Ní Shuilleabháin, 'Marriage, Divorce and Stagnation in the Irish Conflict of Laws' 52(2) *Irish Jurist* 68 (2014).
503. [2017] IESC 40.
504. This recognition will not be lost or withdrawn if the husband contracts a further marriage.

> Under the rules of private international law, recognition of a marriage entered into in compliance with a foreign legal system should be refused only if refusal is required for the protection of the values and principles represented in our public policy .... In my view there is no ... harm or threat in the case of a couple living in this State in a monogamous relationship, arising purely out of the fact that they married under a system of law that permits polygamy. There is no principle at stake here, no damage to the core values of our constitutional concept of marriage, that could be said to require the withholding of recognition.[505]

247. An actually polygamous marriage, however, remains highly unlikely to receive legal recognition. The Supreme Court expressed its view (albeit obiter) that 'marriage, as far as the Constitution is concerned, must in all cases be seen as a union between two people'.[506] Consequently, in its opinion, any second or subsequent marriage entered into while the marriage to a first wife is in being cannot be recognised as valid in Irish law.[507] Despite this, however, the court added that 'this does not necessarily mean that such a marriage can never have legal consequences'.[508] While the Department of Justice was understood to be considering legislative intervention on the issue, no such reform appears to have materialised.[509]

248. Reflecting on the decision, Ní Shúilleabháin notes that 'Irish law has shifted gear, from a position of unthinking hostility towards overseas Islamic marriage to a policy of rational, tolerant accommodation.'[510] Having allowed 'the nonsensical aversion to "potential polygamy" to go unchallenged for far too long', she notes:

> The Irish courts now appear to be determined to honour their human rights commitments and to avoid limping marriages ... unless there is a cogent basis for refusal of recognition. The *HAH v SAA* judgment also suggests a willingness to combine an ideological commitment to gender equality with some practical concessions to the 'lived reality' of polygamy – although the court fell short in articulating a theoretical framework for this recognition strategy.[511]

249. Whatever this progress with regard to foreign marriage recognition, it has also been highlighted that difficulties are liable to arise in relation to the recognition of

505. [2017] IESC 40 at [105].
506. [2017] IESC 40 at [113].
507. At *HAH v. SAA & ors* [2017] IESC 40 at [115], the court noted that 'recognition of an actually polygamous marriage would be contrary to a fundamental constitutional principle and therefore contrary to public policy'.
508. [2017] IESC 40 at [121].
509. Colm Kenna, 'Call for Legal Clarity on Rights of Polygamous Families' *Irish Times*, 16 Jun. 2017.
510. Máire Ní Shuilleabháin, 'Overseas Marriage and Divorce in Islamic Form: A Critical Perspective on the Development of Irish Private International Law' in Kathryn O'Sullivan (ed.) *Minority Religions under Irish Law: Islam in National and International Context* 131, 154 (Brill, 2019).
511. Máire Ní Shuilleabháin, 'Overseas Marriage and Divorce in Islamic Form: A Critical Perspective on the Development of Irish Private International Law' in Kathryn O'Sullivan (ed.) *Minority Religions under Irish Law: Islam in National and International Context* 131, 154 (Brill, 2019).

foreign divorces, particularly Islamic divorces.[512] Pursuant to section 5(1) of the Domicile and Recognition of Foreign Divorces Act 1986, overseas divorces granted in the jurisdiction of domicile of either spouse are recognised, where neither spouse was domiciled either in the granting jurisdiction or in Ireland under section 5(4). Despite this, the extent to which recognition would be afforded to private divorces conducted overseas, such as a bare Islamic talak, remains unclear, given that the legislation appears to contemplate the recognition of divorces granted by courts.[513] Considering the rapid growth of the Irish Muslim community in recent times, the need for urgent clarification of such issues appears tacit. As Ní Shúilleabháin argues:

> There is … a clear need for domestic legislative reform, given the inflexibility of the 1986 Act – and its inadaptability to Islamic divorce norms. The existing legal vacuum is indefensible in a context of substantial immigration from Muslim majority countries.[514]

250. What is clear, however, is that progress (albeit slow) is being made. Following the Thirty-eighth Amendment of the Constitution in May 2019, Article 41.3.3°, which regulates the recognition of foreign divorces at a constitutional level, was amended. It now states: 'Provision may be made by law for the recognition under the law of the State of a dissolution of marriage granted under the civil law of another state.'[515] This amendment appears to be the first step in a more sweeping reform of the law in relation to the recognition of foreign divorces. While discrete areas of law have been clarified through the enactment of the Family Law Act 2019 to make provision for the recognition of divorces, legal separations and marriage annulments granted under UK law, more reforming initiatives are expected in the near future.[516] However, whether the issue of Islamic divorce, specifically, will be addressed remains unclear.

---

512. *See* Máire Ní Shuilleabháin, 'Overseas Marriage and Divorce in Islamic Form: A Critical Perspective on the Development of Irish Private International Law' in Kathryn O'Sullivan (ed.) *Minority Religions under Irish Law: Islam in National and International Context* 131 (Brill, 2019); Máire Ní Shuilleabháin, 'Foreign Divorce Recognition and Residence: A Critical Analysis of H v H' 57 *Irish Jurist* 162 (2017); Máire Ní Shuilleabháin, 'Marriage, Divorce and Stagnation in the Irish Conflict of Laws' 52(2) *Irish Jurist* 68 (2014); Avril Cryan, 'Changing Demographics: Legal Responses to Polygamy and the Challenges Ahead for Ireland' 19(4) *Irish Journal of Family Law* 82 (2016). Note, pursuant to the Brussels II *bis* Regulation, EU Member State divorces are afforded automatic recognition. However, for non-EU divorces, Irish legislation continues to play an important role.
513. The Act refers to the 'grant' of divorce and the 'institution of proceedings'.
514. Máire Ní Shuilleabháin, 'Overseas Marriage and Divorce in Islamic Form: A Critical Perspective on the Development of Irish Private International Law' in Kathryn O'Sullivan (ed.) *Minority Religions under Irish Law: Islam in National and International Context* 131, 154 (Brill, 2019).
515. It previously stated: 'No person whose marriage has been dissolved under the civil law of any other State but is a subsisting valid marriage under the law for the time being in force within the jurisdiction of the Government and Parliament established by this Constitution shall be capable of contracting a valid marriage within that jurisdiction during the lifetime of the other party to the marriage so dissolved.'
516. In 2019, the then Minister for Justice, Charlie Flanagan, indicated that he intended to legislate to introduce greater consistency in the recognition of foreign divorces, *see* http://www.justice.ie/en/JELR/Pages/PR19000192 (accessed 24 Jul. 2019). Note, the Law Reform Commission has also included an examination of recognition of foreign divorces in its Fifth Programme of Law Reform.

Chapter 2. Legal Position of Religious Family Law

251. It has been noted that '[h]istorically, the courts were very slow to interfere with the upbringing of a child and traditionally family law only focused on the issue of child custody and access in the context of marital disputes or where an unmarried parent sought access or guardianship in respect of the child'.[517] Reflecting this approach, significant autonomy is afforded to parents under the Irish Constitution with regard (as discussed in Part IX) to the education and upbringing of children. Recognising the family as 'the primary and natural educator of the child', the State guarantees through Article 42 to 'respect the inalienable right and duty of parents' to provide for the religious as well as moral, intellectual, physical and social education of their children. Given these protections for the family, as Crowley observes, 'for the most part, the State cannot interfere in the decisions made by the family in respect of the formation and/or upbringing of the children'.[518] However, notwithstanding this, it is clear that the Irish legislature and courts will act to protect children who are deemed to be in danger.[519]

252. With the Thirty-First Amendment of the Constitution in 2012, the rights of the child, specifically, have received heightened constitutional protection. Article 42A.1 provides: 'The State recognises and affirms the natural and imprescriptible rights of all children and shall, as far as practicable, by its laws protect and vindicate those rights.' The Constitution also reaffirms in Article 42A.4 that the best interests of the child 'shall be the paramount consideration' in proceedings involving issues such as adoption, guardianship, custody or access. In such scenarios, it adds that the views of 'any child who is capable of forming his or her own views … shall be ascertained and given due weight having regard to the age and maturity of the child'.[520]

253. While the implications of these provisions have yet to be teased out in the superior courts, it has been observed that 'the courts have repeatedly shown a willingness to establish numerous implied or unenumerated rights of the child'.[521] In the 1980 decision of *G v. An Bord Uchtála*, as well as recognising a child's right to bodily integrity, O'Higgins CJ also recognised the child's right: 'to rest and recreation, to the practice of religion, and to follow his or her conscience … The child's natural right to life and all that flows from that right are independent of any right of the parent as such'.[522]

517. Louise Crowley, *Family Law* 97 (Roundhall, 2013).
518. Louise Crowley, *Family Law* 97–98 (Roundhall, 2013).
519. Note, also, s. 3 of the Status of Children Act 1987 states 'the relationship between every person and his father and mother (or either of them) shall, unless the contrary intention appears, be determined irrespective of whether his father and mother are or have been married to each other, and all other relationships shall be determined accordingly'.
520. Article 42A.4.2°.
521. Louise Crowley, *Family Law* 202 (Roundhall, 2013).
522. [1980] 1 IR 32 at 69.

254. In all disputes or applications concerning guardianship, custody of, or access to any child, the 'best interests' of the child will be the chief consideration as mandated by Article 42A.4.1° of the Irish Constitution. Pursuant to section 3(1) of the Guardianship of Infants Act 1964, where, in any proceedings before any court, the guardianship, custody or upbringing of, or access to, a child, 'is in question, the court, in deciding that question, shall regard the best interests of the child as the paramount consideration'. In determining the best interests of the child, Part V of the Act requires the court to 'have regard to all of the factors or circumstances that it regards as relevant to the child concerned and his or her family including matters such as 'the child's religious, spiritual, cultural and linguistic upbringing and needs'.

255. Finally, it would be remiss not to note recent changes in relation to the law on abortion, previously discussed in Part VII Chapter 6. In 1983, the Eighth Amendment of the Constitution Act amended Article 40.3 to acknowledge the right to life of the unborn, with due regard to the equal right to life of the mother. In effect, this resulted in a ban on abortion unless there was a risk to the life (as distinct from health) of the mother. Since the passing of the 2018 referendum on the Thirty-Sixth Amendment to the Constitution, however, the so-called Eighth Amendment has been repealed. The newly introduced Health (Regulation of Termination of Pregnancy) Act 2018 now permits abortion services to be provided in Ireland in three core situations: where there is a risk to the life, or of serious harm to the health, of the pregnant woman; where there is a condition likely to lead to the death of foetus; or in early pregnancy, not exceeding twelve weeks gestation.[523]

523. *See* Part VII Ch. 6 above for more.

Part XI. Religion and Culture

Introduction

256. This part considers the relationship between religion and culture from a legal perspective in Ireland. As discussed in Part VII Chapter 3, Article 40.6.1° of the Irish Constitution provides that the State guarantees liberty for the rights of the citizens to freely express their convictions and opinions 'subject to public order and morality'. The second reference highlights the State's constitutionally recognised role of ensuring that 'organs of public opinion, such as the radio, the press, the cinema, while preserving their rightful liberty of expression,' do not undermine public order or morality. Notwithstanding the removal in 2019 of the constitutional offence of blasphemy,[524] the 'censorious tone'[525] of the provision remains apparent in Article 40.6.1°.i which states: 'The publication or utterance of seditious or indecent matter is an offence which shall be punishable in accordance with law.'

257. Building on the discussion of freedom of expression in Part VII Chapter 3, this part explores the legal framework regulating religion, art and media – an area that has attracted considerable legislative attention in Ireland for almost a hundred years. The part then continues with an exploration of how religion and civil society interact, placing a focus on issues of chaplaincy and the facilitation of religious dietary preferences, in particular. Finally, the part concludes with a consideration of the place of religion in Irish public debate.

---

524. *See* Part VII Ch. 3.
525. Eoin Carolan & Ailbhe O'Neill, *Media Law in Ireland* 65 (2nd ed., Bloomsbury Professional, 2019).

Chapter 1. Religion and Art

§1. Introduction

258. Notwithstanding recent reforms removing the constitutionally recognised offence of blasphemy,[526] numerous legislative enactments continue, to a greater or lesser extent, to impact religion, the freedom of expression and the arts in Ireland. In this regard, the Censorship of Films Act 1923 (as amended), the Video Recordings Acts 1989–1992 and the Censorship of Publications Acts 1929–1967 are particularly worthy of note.

§2. Censorship of Films

259. The Censorship of Films Act 1923 (as amended) continues to play a role in the regulation of films in Ireland. The 1923 Act established the Film Censors Office – renamed in 2008 the Irish Film Classification Office (IFCO) – and lays down the general framework for film classification, which applies in the jurisdiction today.[527] Pursuant to the 1923 Act (as amended), no picture shall be exhibited in public unless the Director of Film Classification, formerly known as the Film Censor, has certified that it is suitable and a certificate is displayed to that effect. Section 7(2) of the Act (as amended) provides:

> the [Director of Film Classification] shall certify the picture unless he is of the opinion that such picture or some part thereof is unfit for general exhibition in public by reason of its being indecent or obscene or because the exhibition thereof in public would tend to inculcate principles contrary to public morality or would be otherwise subversive of public morality.[528]

260. Where concerns are raised, the 1923 Act (as amended) also empowers the Director of Film Classification to prohibit a picture or to impose conditions or restrictions upon its exhibition.

261. The Classification of Films Appeal Board, formerly known as the Censorship of Films Appeal Board, is also established under the Censorship of Films Act 1923 (as amended). This Board consists of nine members appointed by the Minister and has the power to reverse or vary a decision of the Director of Film Classification. Its decision is binding, and where an appeal is successful, a certificate must be granted. Where, further to an unsuccessful appeal, an appellant wishes to challenge

526. *See* Part VII Ch. 3.
527. *See*, http://www.ifco.ie/ (accessed 29 Jul. 2019). IFCO note: 'This short and remarkably succinct piece of legislation, although drafted during the silent movie era, remains the basis upon which IFCO operates today.' *See*, http://www.ifco.ie/en/ifco/pages/legislation (accessed 29 Jul. 2019).
528. Note, this section was most recently amended by s. 2 of the Blasphemy (Abolition of Offences and Related Matters) Act 2019.

the decision of the Classification of Films Appeal Board, this may be pursued by way of judicial review.[529]

262. Historically, the Film Censors Office played an active role in censorship.[530] Monty Python's Life of Brian, released world-wide in 1979, was initially banned in Ireland and was not certified until 1987. Similarly, Monty Python's The Meaning of Life was prohibited from distribution in 1983 and not released until 1990. Although rarely intervening in modern times, the role of the IFCO in film censorship does continue to occasionally attract attention. In 2016, the distributor behind Louis Theroux's documentary My Scientology Movie confirmed that it would not be seeking a release in Ireland.[531] Although Ireland's blasphemy and censorship laws were widely blamed for the decision – with multiple outlets (wrongly) suggesting that the documentary was subject to a 'ban'[532] – it appears the distributors had not sought classification from the Director of Film Classification.[533] Whether due to the deterrent effect of the Irish framework or driven by other unrelated factors, the decision nevertheless added to the perception of the continuing importance of censorship in Ireland. This image is one which the IFCO seems keen to change, continually seeking to place the focus on its responsibility for the certification of movies as opposed to its previous role as a film censor.[534]

§3. Censorship of Video Recordings

263. The Video Recordings Acts 1989–1992 effectively extended film censorship to 'video work' defined in section 1 as:

> any series of visual images (whether with or without sound)–
>
> (a) produced, whether electronically or by other means, by the use of information contained on any disc or magnetic tape, and
> (b) shown as a moving picture'.

---

529. *See* Eoin Carolan & Ailbhe O'Neill, *Media Law in Ireland* 94–97 (2nd ed., Bloomsbury Professional, 2019) for more.
530. *See* Kevin Rockett, *Irish Film Censorship: A Cultural Journey from Silent Cinema to Internet Pornography* (Four Courts Press, 2004) for a historical overview of film censorship in Ireland. *See also* Marie McGonagle, *Media Law* 315–318 (2nd ed., Roundhall, 2003).
531. 'Blasphemy row. No Irish release for Scientology film' (RTÉ News, 27 Sep. 2016).
532. 'Blasphemy row. No Irish release for Scientology film' (RTÉ News, 27 Sep. 2016). *See also* https://www.theransomnote.com/culture/news/louis-therouxs-scientology-documentary-banned-in-ireland/ (accessed 29 Jul. 2019).
533. Neville Cox highlighted several reasons why the blasphemy laws were of no relevance. He explained that the State does not define the Church of Scientology as a religion with charitable status and that, for blasphemy, the material complained of has to deal with issues held sacred by a 'religion'. He also noted that, as a documentary, it would likely be considered of literary, political, artistic or scientific merit and thus not blasphemous. *See* Donald Clarke, 'Why Ireland Won't "Ban" Louis Theroux's Scientology Film' *Irish Times*, 27 Sep. 2016.
534. The rebranding of the office and role of director, casting aside the use of the word 'censor', is one such example. IFCO has also sought to be more transparent and user-friendly, *see* Joe Humphries, 'Website to Give Reasons for Film Censor's Decisions' *Irish Times*, 3 Sep. 2004.

264. The Acts provide that the Director of Film Classification shall certify a video work as fit for viewing unless, for example, the viewing of it would be likely to stir up hatred against a group of persons in the State or elsewhere on account of their religion.[535]

265. As with films, the Director of Film Classification may make a prohibition order in relation to a video where it is deemed unfit for viewing having regard to this test.[536] Subject to certain exceptions, a person who supplies or offers to supply a video recording containing a video work in respect of which a prohibition order is in force;[537] who is in possession of it for the purposes of supplying it to another;[538] who exhibits it other than in a private dwelling;[539] or who imports it into the State without a permit[540] shall be guilty of an offence.

266. Although technically, video games are exempt from classification under the Video Recordings Act 1989, pursuant to section 3(1) of the 1989 Act, it appears the Director of Film Classification may also be able to prohibit a video game if it is judged unfit for viewing.

§4. Censorship of Publications

267. The Censorship of Publications Acts 1929–1967 continue to regulate the censorship of publications in Ireland. The Censorship of Publications Board, established under the Censorship of Publications Act 1946, comprises five members appointed by the Minister for Justice. A complaint may be made to the Censorship of Publications Board by any person, or the Board may examine a book of its own

---

535. Section 3(1)(a) states that the Director of Film Classification shall certify a video work as fit for viewing unless:

(a) the viewing of it–
   (i) would be likely to cause persons to commit crimes, whether by inciting or encouraging them to do so or by indicating or suggesting ways of doing so or of avoiding detection, or
   (ii) would be likely to stir up hatred against a group of persons in the State or elsewhere on account of their race, colour, nationality, religion, ethnic or national origins, membership of the travelling community or sexual orientation, or
   (iii) would tend, by reason of the inclusion in it of obscene or indecent matter, to deprave or corrupt persons who might view it,
   Or
(b) it depicts acts of gross violence or cruelty (including mutilation and torture) towards humans or animals.

536. Section 7.
537. Section 8.
538. Section 9.
539. Section 11.
540. Section 16.

choosing.[541] Pursuant to section 6(2) of the Censorship of Publications Act 1946, when examining a book, the Censorship Board shall have regard to:

(a) the literary, artistic, scientific or historic merit or importance, and the general tenor of the book;
(b) the language in which it is written;
(c) the nature and extent of the circulation which, in their opinion, it is likely to have;
(d) the class of reader which, in their opinion, may reasonably be expected to read it;
(e) any other matter relating to the book which appears to them to be relevant.

268. Moreover, the Board may communicate with the author, editor or publisher of the book and may take into account any representation made by him in relation thereto.[542] Where a book is regarded as 'indecent or obscene', it may be prohibited.[543] Although 'obscene' remains undefined in legislation, 'indecent' is defined in section 1 of the 1946 Act as including 'suggestive of, or inciting to, sexual immorality or unnatural vice or likely in any other similar way to corrupt or deprave'.

269. The Censorship of Publications Appeal Board, established under section 3 of the Censorship of Publications Act 1946, deals with appeals from the Censorship of Publications Board. Appeals against a prohibition order may be taken by the author, editor, or publisher of the publication or any five members of the Oireachtas acting jointly.[544] Akin to the Censorship of Publications Board, it also consists of five members, including a chairperson who must be a judge of the Supreme Court, High Court or Circuit Court or a practising solicitor or barrister with no less than seven years' standing. Albeit not explicitly stated at a legislative level, appeals of this Board's decision may be taken by way of judicial review.[545]

270. Similar to the Film Censors Office, the Censorship of Publications Board played an active role in censorship in Ireland throughout much of the twentieth century.[546] While the Censorship of Publications Board is not required to divulge its rationale for the banning of any book, nor is the Board expressly required to have regard to religious considerations in determining whether or not to ban a publication, the influence of the Roman Catholic Church, in particular, in supporting the

541. The Board will only examine periodicals where there is a complaint from a member of the public. Note also the role of Customs officials in referring books to the Censorship Board as highlighted in s. 5 of the 1946 Act.
542. Section 6(3) of the 1946 Act. For more, *see* Eoin Carolan & Ailbhe O'Neill, *Media Law in Ireland* 88–94 (2nd ed., Bloomsbury Professional, 2019).
543. Section 7.
544. Note, complaints and appeals must be made in accordance with the Censorship of Publications Regulations 1980.
545. Eoin Carolan & Ailbhe O'Neill, *Media Law in Ireland* 93 (2nd ed., Bloomsbury Professional, 2019).
546. For more on the history of censorship of publications, *see* Marie McGonagle, *Media Law* 318–323 (2nd ed. Roundhall, 2003).

introduction of the governing legislation has been recognised.[547] Although its visibility has been dramatically reduced in recent decades, in 2016, the Board unanimously chose to ban the publication in Ireland of Jean Martin's The Raped Little Runaway. It was the first ban on a publication in eighteen years and reopened the debate as to the role of censorship in modern Ireland.[548]

547. *See* Maurice Curtis, *A Challenge to Democracy: Militant Catholicism in Modern Ireland* (The History Press, 2010). Note, also, criticisms of the Catholic Church were widely believed to have played a role in the 1958 ban applied to Brendan Behan's *Borstal Boy*, *see* Nuala McCann, *Between the Sheets: Banned Books Censors Didn't Want You to Read* (BBC, 4 Nov. 2016). Considering the role of censorship in Ireland, Anthony Keating, 'The Uses and Abuses of Censorship: God, Ireland and the Battle to Extend Censorship Post 1929' 9 *Estudios Irlandes* 67 (2014) argues that 'religio-nationalist ideologues' sought to protect the Irish people from 'spiritual and intellectual contaminants', noting that the 'main source of these "contaminants" came in the shape of the cinema … and the published word'. *See also* Anthony Keating, 'Censorship the Cornerstone of Catholic Ireland' 57(2) *Journal of Church and State* 289 (2015).

548. Ed Power, 'Repulsive Book, But Is Censorship Right?' *Irish Independent*, 20 Mar. 2016. *See also* Gordon Deegan, '"Vile" Banned Book Contained Five Sex Acts on Girl in First 77 Pages, Ennis Court Told' *Irish Times*, 28 Jun. 2019 which reports on a prosecution taken against a person found in possession of the book.

Chapter 2. Religion and Media

§1. Press Regulation

271. Ireland adopts a hybrid model of press regulation which involves elements of both statutory and self-regulation.[549] The Office of the Press Ombudsman and the Press Council of Ireland, both of which are independent bodies, enjoy statutory status under the Defamation Act 2009.[550] The Code of Practice for Newspapers and Periodicals, which they enforce, however, was devised by the Press Industry Steering Committee.[551] The Office of the Press Ombudsman and the Press Council of Ireland are, moreover, funded by the press industry.

272. Principle 8 of the Code, enforced by the Press Ombudsman and the Press Council of Ireland, states that the press shall not publish material intended or likely to cause grave offence or stir up hatred against an individual or group on the basis of various features, including religion.[552] A number of cases have been brought before the Ombudsman claiming violation of this principle.[553] In 2015, the Ambassador of Israel made a formal complaint to the Press Ombudsman's Office in relation to an article published in the Irish Times, which he argued was responsible for stirring up hatred against the 'Jewish State of Israel', thus breaching Principle 8.[554] In explaining its decision to reject the complaint, the Press Ombudsman's Office observed:

> To sustain an argument that Principle 8 has been breached it is necessary to argue that the State of Israel can be coterminous with a race, religion, nationality or ethnic origin. It is my view that the State of Israel does not conform to any of these groups and therefore I can find no breach of Principle 8.[555]

273. The Office continued:

> To accept that the State of Israel can be defined by race, religion, nationality or ethnic origin is to ignore the multiplicity of races, religions, nationalities and

549. *See* Eoin Carolan & Ailbhe O'Neill, *Media Law in Ireland* 547–551 (2nd ed., Bloomsbury Professional, 2019). They note this approach was adopted to avoid the weaknesses of either an exclusively self-regulatory or regulatory model. The adoption of a regulatory model was supported by the *Report of the Legal Advisory Group on Defamation* (2003).
550. *See* http://www.presscouncil.ie/ (accessed 30 Jul. 2019).
551. Thus, although the Irish Government does not technically censor or control the press in Ireland, certain professional standards and behaviours are required of the print media.
552. *See* http://www.presscouncil.ie/press-council-of-ireland-1/code-of-practice- (accessed 30 Jul. 2019). Note, how s. 26(2) of the Defamation Act 2009 strongly incentivises publications to become members of the Press Council and abide by the Code of Practice.
553. For more on how complaints may be made to the Ombudsman, *see* Eoin Carolan & Ailbhe O'Neill, *Media Law in Ireland* 552–554 (2nd ed., Bloomsbury Professional, 2019).
554. *See* http://www.presscouncil.ie/his-excellency-boaz-modai-ambassador-of-israel-and-the-irish-times-2452 (accessed 30 Jul. 2019).
555. *See* http://www.presscouncil.ie/his-excellency-boaz-modai-ambassador-of-israel-and-the-irish-times-2452 (accessed 30 Jul. 2019).

> ethnic groups that are found in Israel. It is also to deny the distinction between the State and its people. One can be critical of a State's activities and policies without in any way being critical of its people.[556]

274. Subsequently, in 2018, a complaint was received in relation to a cartoon published in the Sunday Independent in the aftermath of the abortion referendum – the Thirty-Sixth Amendment to the Constitution.[557] Although it was claimed that the cartoon was in breach of Principle 8, given its offensive nature to Catholics, the Press Ombudsman's Office again rejected the complaint. It noted that while there was 'no doubt that the cartoon offended some people', there is 'a degree of licence available to cartoons to engage in ridicule, satire and irony which is not available to other forms of journalism'. It concluded that '[f]or this reason, any offence caused by the cartoon did not breach Principle 8 of the Code of Practice'.[558]

§2. Regulation of Broadcast Media

275. The broadcast media in Ireland is regulated by the Broadcasting Authority of Ireland (BAI). Part 2 of the Broadcasting Act 2009 provides for the establishment of the Authority, comprising nine members appointed for a five-year term,[559] and sets out its broad remit. Among the objectives of the Authority as stated under section 25(1) are that it shall endeavour to ensure:

> that the number and categories of broadcasting services made available in the State … best serve the needs of the people of the island of Ireland, bearing in mind their languages and traditions and their *religious, ethical and cultural diversity*.[560]

276. Section 114(3) of the 2009 Act provides that RTÉ, the leading Irish public service broadcaster, shall ensure that its broadcast services:

> provide a comprehensive range of programmes in the Irish and English languages that *reflect the cultural diversity* of the whole island of Ireland and

556. *See* http://www.presscouncil.ie/his-excellency-boaz-modai-ambassador-of-israel-and-the-irish-times-2452 (accessed 30 Jul. 2019). Reflecting on a different complaint lodged in 2015, again by the Ambassador of Israel against the *Irish Times*, the Press Ombudsman's Office noted: 'An accusation of anti-Semitism about a reporter is a serious matter and if found to be true could possibly be a breach of Principle 8.' In the circumstances, however, no such evidence was found. *See* http://www.presscouncil.ie/his-excellency-boaz-modai-ambassador-of-israel-and-the-irish-times-2453 (accessed 30 Jul. 2019).

557. *See* http://www.presscouncil.ie/about-us/recent-decisions-and-news/a-man-and-the-sunday-independent- (accessed 30 Jul. 2019). The cartoon showed a surgeon in an operating theatre removing a set of rosary beads from a female patient in a hospital bed with a caption referring to a 'rosarectomy'.

558. *See* http://www.presscouncil.ie/about-us/recent-decisions-and-news/a-man-and-the-sunday-independent- (accessed 30 Jul. 2019).

559. Members can be reappointed for no more than two consecutive terms, *see* s. 9(5) of the 2009 Act.

560. Section 25(1)(a) of the 2009 Act (emphasis added). *See* s. 26 for the functions of the BAI.

> include programmes that … provide coverage of … *religious* and cultural activities and cater for the expectations of the community generally as well as members of the community with special or minority interests … .[561]

277. This obligation is met, for example, by the daily coverage of Roman Catholic mass on its RTÉ News Now channel. It also broadcasts weekly Christian masses and services on Sundays. Other religious content involves a mix of 'in-house' and commissioned programming.[562] In terms of in-house productions, short films marking minority faith festivals are supported alongside longer-running documentary series such as Would You Believe? which itself covers a broad range of religious and spiritual subjects.

278. It is worthwhile to note that section 71(6) of the Broadcasting Act 2009 empowers the BAI to terminate a contract provision where any of the programme material supplied in pursuance of the contract contravenes, among others, the Prohibition of Incitement to Hatred Act 1989. The Authority are, moreover, legislatively compelled to terminate such a contract where such contravention has occurred at least twice within six months. As per its designation, the 1989 Act prohibits incitement to hatred, with 'hatred' defined as referring to hatred against a group of persons in the State or elsewhere on account, among others, of their religion.[563]

§3. Advertising

279. Advertising in Ireland is governed by various pieces of legislation, including the Indecent Advertisements Act 1889, the Censorship of Publications Act 1929 and the Broadcasting Act 2009. The Advertising Standards Authority for Ireland (ASAI), moreover, is an independent self-regulatory body set up and financed by the advertising industry.[564] It produces the Code of Standards for Advertising and Marketing Communications in Ireland, which is drawn up by the Board of ASAI following detailed consultation with all relevant interest groups, including the public, advertisers, agencies and media, consumer representatives and Government departments. The

561. (Emphasis added) Note, TG4, another public service broadcaster, is subject to similar requirements under s. 118.
562. RTÉ note: 'Because of the Religious Genre's in-house production capacity, commissioning opportunities on both TV and Radio are limited, but not non-existent. On radio, because of *The Leap of Faith's* presence in the schedule from October to May, only ideas likely to attract BAI and/or other third party funding will be considered. While fully funded TV proposals will be considered, ideas that attract finance from other broadcasters or funding bodies are, of course, desirable.' *See* https://about.rte.ie/commissioning/commissioning-briefs/rte-religion-2/ (accessed 1 Nov. 2023).
563. *See* s. 1 of the Prohibition of Incitement to Hatred Act 1989. Broadcasts likely to stir up hatred are addressed in s. 3 albeit that s. 5 provides an exception where fair and accurate reporting of proceedings of the *Oireachtas* or judicial proceedings are involved.
564. *See* https://www.asai.ie/ (accessed 30 Jul. 2019).

Code applies to commercial marketing communications and to sales promotions that promote the sales of goods or services.[565] Pursuant to the 7th Edition of the Code of Standards for Advertising and Marketing Communications in Ireland, which came into effect on 1 March 2016, the ASAI note:

> Marketing communications should respect the dignity of all persons and should avoid causing offence on grounds of gender, marital or civil status, family status, sexual orientation, *religion*, age, disability, race or membership of the Traveller community.[566]

280. Moreover, it notes:

> To avoid causing offence, marketing communications should be responsive to the diversity in Irish society and marketing communications which portray or refer to minority groups or vulnerable people should … *Not ridicule or exploit religious beliefs, symbols, rites or practices.*[567]

281. The BAI, the regulator of broadcasting in Ireland, also produces codes of conduct in relation to advertising.[568]

282. Religious advertising specifically is subject to special legislative controls in Ireland with a blanket ban on such advertising formerly applied in the jurisdiction. Section 20(4) of the Broadcasting Act 1960 prohibited RTÉ, the national broadcaster, from accepting any advertisement which was directed towards any religious end.[569] This prohibition was effectively extended to all independent broadcasters under the Radio and Television Act 1988.[570] Notwithstanding its obvious intrusion on the freedom of expression, the ban was upheld as constitutional by the IESC in *Murphy v. IRTC*[571] and was subsequently deemed 'necessary in a democratic society' by the ECtHR in *Murphy v. Ireland.*[572]

283. The prohibition in relation to religious advertising has been somewhat relaxed in modern times, however. First, section 65 of the Broadcasting Act 2001 confirmed that nothing in section 20(4) of the 1960 Act or section 10(3) of the 1988 Act:

565. The Code is available at https://www.asai.ie/asaicode/ (accessed 30 Jul. 2019). It does not cover non-commercial marketing communications, such as those which express the advertiser's position on, for example, religious matters.
566. Rule 3.17 (emphasis added).
567. Rule 3.19(e) (emphasis added).
568. *See* https://www.bai.ie/en/codes-standards/#al-block-7 (accessed 1 Nov. 2023).
569. Note, political advertising or advertising pertaining to industrial disputes was also prohibited.
570. *See* s. 10(3).
571. [1999] 1 IR 12.
572. (2004) 38 EHRR 13. For a critique of the Murphy litigation, *see* Eoin Carolan & Ailbhe O'Neill, *Media Law in Ireland* 75–79 (2nd ed., Bloomsbury Professional, 2019).

shall be construed as preventing the broadcasting of a notice of the fact–

(a) that a particular religious newspaper, magazine or periodical is available for sale or supply, or
(b) that any event or ceremony associated with any particular religion will take place, if the contents of the notice do not address the issue of the merits or otherwise of adhering to any religious faith or belief or of becoming a member of any religion or religious organisation.

284. Second, section 41(4) of the Broadcasting Act 2009 now provides a narrower prohibition on religious advertising than that formerly applied, stating:

> A broadcaster shall not broadcast an advertisement which addresses the issue of the merits or otherwise of adhering to any religious faith or belief or of becoming a member of any religion or religious organisation.[573]

573. It has been observed that this provision 'seems to be targeted primarily at proselytising' and is 'a lessor interference with freedom of expression' than the earlier bans. *See* Eoin Carolan & Ailbhe O'Neill, *Media Law in Ireland* 75 (2nd ed., Bloomsbury Professional, 2019).

Chapter 3. Religion and Civil Society

§1. Introduction

285. Religious organisations and institutions, most notably the Roman Catholic Church, continue to play a prominent role in Irish society. In addition to the denominational schools' system applied in the jurisdiction,[574] various hospitals and other institutions providing public service remain under the patronage of named religions. Religious organisations also play a key role in supporting the homeless and the poor and often provide vital social services to those most in need. For the purposes of this chapter, a focus will be placed on some lesser-known roles played by chaplains[575] and religious representatives in Irish public life. The chapter will also consider how the need to facilitate religious dietary preferences has, in certain contexts, been recognised by Irish law.

§2. Prison Chaplaincy

286. The 'religious, spiritual and moral life' of prisoners is directly addressed within the Prison Rules 2007.[576] Rule 34(1) provides:

> Each prisoner shall, in so far as is practicable and subject to the maintenance of good order and safe and secure custody, be permitted to practice and comply with the rules, observances and norms of behaviour of the religious denomination of which he or she is a follower or member.[577]

287. Moreover, subject to certain conditions (relating, for example, to the maintenance of good order), 'each prisoner shall be permitted to have access to, for his or her own use, religious books, items and materials relating to the religious faith of which he or she is a follower or member'.[578] Subject to similar constraints, each prisoner 'may attend such services or meetings in the prison of his or her denomination as may, with the consent of the Governor, be arranged by a chaplain, or any person approved for this purpose by a religious denomination'.[579] Although the Rules provide that no prisoner shall be compelled to meet with a chaplain[580] (nor to attend any religious service or meeting),[581] they equally provide that a prisoner shall

574. *See* Part IX.
575. *See* above Part VII and Part IX for more. Note, in particular, the discussion in Part VIII regarding the Supreme Court decision in *Campaign to Separate Church and State v. Minister for Education* [1998] 3 IR 321 where the payment of chaplains was not regarded as endowment of a religion.
576. Pursuant to Rule 4(i), where a prisoner is admitted into prison and his or her particulars are recorded, his or her religious denomination (if any) is noted. Rule 34(2) states that where a prisoner converts to a particular religious denomination or renounces the religious denomination which is recorded for them in their prisoner details, their details shall be amended accordingly.
577. For the facilitation of religious dietary requirements, *see* below.
578. Rule 34(3).
579. Rule 34(4).
580. Rule 34(8).
581. Rule 34(5).

not, in so far as is practicable, be refused access to a chaplain of any religious denomination whether the prisoner is a member of the denomination or not.[582] Where a prisoner meets with a chaplain, subject to certain limitations, the meeting 'shall not … be held in the presence or view, or within the hearing, of a prison officer unless the chaplain or prisoner concerned so requests'.[583] Cognisant of the needs of prisoners from minority religions, Rule 34(10) provides that a prisoner who belongs to a religious denomination for which there is no authorised chaplain may enjoy visits from a spiritual or pastoral advisor with the permission of the Governor.[584] Such visits are, however, subject to more stringent oversight as they may take place at the discretion of the Governor in the view of but not within the hearing of a prison officer.[585]

288. The duties of prison chaplains are set out in Rule 114 of the Prison Rules 2007. They include the duty to visit prisoners who are willing to be visited or who request a visit; to minister to prisoners of his or her religious denomination; to conduct religious services for prisoners of his or her religious denomination; and, subject to certain conditions, to visit any prisoner who is under restraint or confined to a cell unless the prisoner is unwilling to receive such a visit. In the provision of chaplaincy services, Rule 115 provides that a chaplain shall, for example, encourage prisoners to talk with him or her;[586] bring to the attention of the Governor any matter relating to the well-being of a prisoner or prisoners, or the provision of chaplaincy services;[587] develop and maintain links with appropriate community-based groups or persons who visit prisoners for spiritual or pastoral purposes;[588] and participate in and contribute to multi-disciplinary working in prison for the effective delivery of services.[589] Rule 118 moreover provides that a chaplain shall inform the Governor in writing if he or she 'is of the opinion that the spiritual, moral, mental, emotional or physical state of any prisoner is being significantly impaired by his or her continued imprisonment'.[590]

289. In 2012, the Irish Council for Civil Liberties (ICCL) and the Irish Penal Reform Trust (IPRT) noted that there were twenty full-time and nine part-time

582. Rule 34(6).
583. Rule 34(9).
584. It states: 'Subject to good order and safe and secure custody, a prisoner who belongs to a religious denomination for which there is no authorised chaplain to the prison may, at his or her request and subject to the Governor's written consent, receive spiritual or pastoral visits at such times as the Governor considers appropriate from a minister or other representative of that religious denomination, upon the Governor being informed of the identity of the minister or other representative concerned.'
585. Rule 34(11). Note also, the Rules for Military Prisons and Detention Barracks 1954 (SI 291/1954) include provisions which seek to recognise religious freedom and to prevent indoctrination.
586. Rule 115(c).
587. Rule 115(d).
588. Rule 115(f).
589. Rule 115(g).
590. It adds that the chaplain 'shall make and keep a record of the prisoner's name, the information given to the Governor under this Rule and the date on which he or she so informed the Governor'.

chaplains from the Roman Catholic, the Church of Ireland and Methodist faiths.[591] Although the statutorily mandated annual reports from prison chaplains to the Director General of the Irish Prison Service were routinely made public prior to 2010,[592] for a number of years thereafter, such reports were not released. In this context, the Irish Times sought and secured the release of the annual reports under Freedom of Information legislation.[593] According to the paper, the chaplains highlighted the need for more chaplaincy staff and the 'need to accommodate the spiritual needs of non-Christian prisoners, particularly Muslims'.[594] In responding to the needs of Muslim inmates, the Times did highlight, however, that the Dóchas Centre chaplaincy provided copies of the Koran and prayer mats to Muslim women in custody, while an imam was also reported as visiting the Midlands Prison once a month.[595] In recent times, the annual reports have once again been made publicly available for various prisons across the country.[596] The reports continue to highlight the diverse religious needs of the Irish prison populations and the extent to which such needs are being met. For example, the 2021 Wheatfield Chaplain's Report noted the special dietary and dining arrangements made for Muslim prisoners observing Ramadan,[597] while the Mountjoy[598] and Cloverhill[599] reports both also referred to the provision of religious reading material to prisoners of both Christian and non-Christian faiths.

§3. Healthcare Regulations

290. Regulation 9(1) of the Health Act 2007 (Care and Welfare of Residents In Designated Centres For Older People) Regulations 2013 states that registered providers of nursing home care are required in their operations to have due regard to a number of features of their residents including their religious persuasion and, pursuant to regulation 9(3)(e) are required to facilitate, insofar as is reasonably practicable, the exercise of resident's 'civil, political and religious rights'. Where a resident is approaching the end of their life, regulation 13 of the 2013 Regulations states that registered providers must ensure 'appropriate care and comfort' are given

591. Irish Council for Civil Liberties and the Irish Penal Reform Trust, Know Your Rights: Your Rights as a Prisoner (2012) 16 available at http://www.iprt.ie/files/ICCL_IPRT_Prisoners_rights1.pdf.
592. The production of annual reports by prison chaplains is required under s. 119 of the Prison Rules 2007.
593. *See* Conor Gallagher, 'Prison Is "Wholly Inappropriate" for Mentally Ill People, Say Chaplains' *Irish Times*, 15 Jul. 2019.
594. Conor Gallagher, 'Prison Is "Wholly Inappropriate" for Mentally Ill People, Say Chaplains' *Irish Times*, 15 Jul. 2019.
595. Conor Gallagher, 'Prison Is "Wholly Inappropriate" for Mentally Ill People, Say Chaplains' *Irish Times*, 15 Jul. 2019.
596. *See*, https://www.irishprisons.ie/information-centre/publications/chaplains-reports/ (accessed 1 Nov. 2023).
597. *See*, https://www.irishprisons.ie/wp-content/uploads/documents_pdf/Wheatfield-Annual-Chaplains-Report-2021.pdf at p. 6 (accessed 1 Nov. 2023).
598. *See*, https://www.irishprisons.ie/wp-content/uploads/documents_pdf/Mountjoy-Prison-Annual-Chaplain-Report-2021.pdf at p. 23 (accessed 1 Nov. 2023).
599. *See* https://www.irishprisons.ie/wp-content/uploads/documents_pdf/Cloverhill-Chaplaincy-Service-2021-Annual-Report.pdf at p. 7 (accessed 1 Nov, 2023).

to them to address their 'spiritual needs' and, insofar as is reasonably practicable, that their 'religious and cultural practices' are facilitated.[600]

§4. Religious Dietary Preferences

291. Religious dietary preferences are also recognised in various primary and secondary legislation.[601] Rule 23(2) of the Prison Rules 2007 states:

> Subject to the maintenance of good order and safe and secure custody, the Governor shall, in so far as is practicable ... ensure that provision shall be made to enable a prisoner to observe dietary practices of a religion or culture of which he or she professes to be a follower.[602]

292. Pursuant to regulation 20(3) of the Health Act 2007 (Care and Welfare of Residents In Designated Centres For Older People) Regulations 2009, registered providers of nursing home care should also ensure that any dietary restrictions on religious grounds are facilitated.

600. Schedule 6 of the 2013 Regulations also states that the premises to be provided by registered providers must include a communal space 'suitable for the provision of social, cultural and religious activities appropriate to the circumstances of residents'.
601. For consideration of the recognition of ritual slaughter, *see* Part II.
602. *See* §2 above for how this is reflected within Irish prison, in the facilitation, for example, of Ramadan.

Chapter 4. Religion and Public Debate

293. In many countries across Europe, developments in relation to religion law have dominated public debate. Issues surrounding the wearing of religious headscarves, the use of religious symbols in public buildings and the role of religious tribunals have attracted significant attention. Since the events of 11 September 2001, the perceived threat of extremism and its association with certain religious denominations has, moreover, generated particular media coverage.

294. However, while these debates have led to social divisions and increased religious regulation in many jurisdictions, the Irish experience has been somewhat different. As Sakaranaho has highlighted, the perception among Muslim communities – the largest non-Christian denomination and the third-largest religion in Ireland – appears to be that, given the traditional role of religion in the State, it demonstrates a greater respect for religion than in other European countries.[603] In this context, Fanning observes: 'the visible presence of Muslims in the Republic of Ireland has not become politicised to the extent that it has in several other European countries'.[604] Furthermore, notwithstanding that media attention is occasionally placed on the accommodation of religious headwear in the classroom, hospital and workplace,[605] little debate or case law has emerged on these issues in recent years.

295. Yet, although the increase in multiculturalism in Ireland in recent decades has not given rise to significant conflict nor major state intervention in religion law of the nature observed in other jurisdictions, other pressures have come to bear on religion and the law in Ireland. Of particular note in this regard are the shifts in religious norms which have arisen in Irish society in recent decades. The growth of secularism – or perhaps more accurately, the shift away from Roman Catholicism in Ireland – continues to be a major influencing factor in law and religion in Ireland. Recent referenda on issues such as same-sex marriage,[606] abortion[607] and blasphemy[608] highlight just how these socio-religious changes are impacting Irish law and politics. The very public debates regarding the place of religious education in

603. Tuula Sakaranaho, *Religious Freedom Multiculturalism, Islam: Cross-Reading Finland and Ireland* (Brill, 2006). *See also* Oliver Scharbrodt, 'Muslim Immigration to Ireland after World War II' in Oliver Scharbrodt et al. (eds) *Muslims in Ireland Past and Present* 49–72 (Edinburgh University Press, 2015).

604. Bryan Fanning, *Migration and the Making of Ireland* (UCD Press, 2018). However, James Carr, 'Muslims in Ireland: History, Demographics and Debates' in Kathryn O'Sullivan (ed.) *Minority Religions under Irish Law: Islam in National and International Context* 59, 70 (Brill, 2019) suggests this interpretation is 'debateable'.

605. *See* Claire Hogan, 'The Accommodation of Islam in the Irish Workplace, Classroom and Hospital' in Kathryn O'Sullivan (ed.) *Minority Religions under Irish Law: Islam in National and International Context* 83 (Brill, 2019).

606. *See* Part VII Ch. 2.

607. *See* Part VII Ch. 6.

608. *See* Part VII Ch. 3.

Ireland and the dominance of the Catholic Church in the provision of educational services speak to the continuing tensions which exist.[609]

296. Thus, while various issues continue to generate controversy, most notably the continued fall-out from clerical child sex abuse scandals,[610] it appears likely that future developments in religion and the law in Ireland will be largely motivated by the pressures brought to bear by two key shifts in Irish society: increased multiculturalism and increased secularism. Although it remains unclear how they will be accommodated (and what impact they will have on religious law) in what remains a Catholic-majority country, it appears incontrovertible that the pressures of these socio-religious changes will continue to play an important role in public debate and discourse in the years to come.

609. Although a process of divestment remains ongoing, critics claim the process remains too slow. For discussion of the challenges involved in the divestment of schools, *see* Breda O'Brien, 'Divestment of Schools Requires More to Be Built' *Irish Times*, 6 Apr. 2019.

610. *See* Lydia Buckley, 'Can the Criminal Law Put an End to the "Cover-Up" of Clerical Sexual Abuse?' 24(4) *Irish Criminal Law Journal* 98 (2014). *See also* Susie Donnelly & Tom Inglis, 'The Media and the Catholic Church in Ireland: Reporting Clerical Child Sex Abuse' 25(1) *Journal of Contemporary Religion* 1 (2010).

Selected Bibliography

Books

Bolger, M., Bruton, C. & Kimber, C. *Employment Equality Law*, Dublin: Roundhall, 2012.

Breen, O. & Smith, P. *Law of Charities in Ireland*, Dublin: Bloomsbury, 2019.

Carolan, E. & O'Neill, A. *Media Law in Ireland*, 2nd ed. Dublin: Bloomsbury Professional, 2019.

Crowley, L. *Family Law*, Dublin: Roundhall, 2013.

Curtis, M. A Challenge to Democracy: Militant Catholicism in Modern Ireland, Dublin: The History Press, 2010.

Daly, E. *Religion, Law and the Irish State*, Dublin: Clarus Press, 2012.

Delany, H. & Carolan, E. *The Right to Privacy: A Doctrinal and Comparative Analysis,* Dublin: Thomson Roundhall, 2008.

Doe, N. *Law and Religion in Europe: A Comparative Introduction*, Oxford: OUP, 2011.

Fanning, B. *Migration and the Making of Ireland*, Dublin: UCD Press, 2018.

Fennell, C. *The Law of Evidence in Ireland*, 4th ed. Dublin: Bloomsbury, 2019.

Ferriter, D. *The Border: The Legacy of a Century of Anglo-Irish Politics*, Dublin: Profile Books, 2019.

Fine-Davis, M. *Attitudes to Family Formation in Ireland: Findings from the Nationwide Study,* Dublin: Family Support Agency, 2011.

Haynes, A. & Schweppe, J. *Lifecycle of a Hate Crime: Country Report for Ireland*, Dublin: ICCL, 2017.

Heffernan, L. (with Ní Raifeathaigh, Ú.) *Evidence in Criminal Trials*, Dublin: Bloomsbury Professional, 2014.

Keogh, D. & McCarthy, A. *The Making of the 1937 Constitution,* Cork: Mercer, 2007.

Lindkvist, L. *Religious Freedom and the Universal Declaration of Human Rights*, Cambridge: Cambridge University Press, 2017.

McGonagle, M. *Media Law*, 2nd ed. Dublin: Roundhall, 2003.

Meenan, F. *Employment Law,* Dublin: Roundhall, 2014.

Murphy, A. & Regan, M. *Employment Law,* 2nd ed. Dublin: Bloomsbury, 2017.

O'Malley, T. *Sexual Offences,* 2nd ed. Dublin: Roundhall, 2013.

Rockett, K. *Irish Film Censorship: A Cultural Journey from Silent Cinema to Internet Pornography*, Dublin: Four Courts Press, 2004.

Sakaranaho, T. *Religious Freedom Multiculturalism, Islam: Cross-Reading Finland and Ireland*, Leiden, Netherlands: Brill, 2006.
Siapera, E., Moreo, E. & Zhou, J. *Hate Track: Tracking and Monitoring Racist Speech Online*, Dublin: DCU, 2018.

Edited Books

Carolan, E. & Doyle, O. (eds), *The Irish Constitution: Governance and Values,* Dublin: Roundhall, 2008.
Connolly, L. (ed.), *The 'Irish' Family*, London: Routledge, 2015.
Day, A. (ed.), *Religion and the Individual,* Farnham: Ashgate, 2008.
Devine, F., Lane, F. & Puirséil, N. (eds), *Essays in Irish Labour History. A Festschrift for Elizabeth and John W. Boyle*, Newbridge: Irish Academic Press, 2008.
Fortner, R.S. & Fackler, P.M. (eds), *The Handbook of Global Communication and Media Ethics*, London: Wiley-Blackwell, 2011.
Litton, F. (ed.), *The Constitution of Ireland 1937–1987*, Dublin: Institute of Public Administration, 1988.
Mair, J & Örücü, E. (eds), *The Place of Religion in Family Law*, Cambridge: Intersentia, 2011.
O'Sullivan, K. (ed.), *Minority Religions under Irish Law: Islam in National and International Context,* Leiden, Netherlands: Brill, 2019.
Robbers, G. (ed.), *State and Church in the European Union,* Baden-Baden: Nomos Verlagsgesellshaft, 1996.
Scharbrodt, O. et al (eds), *Muslims in Ireland: Past and Present,* Edinburgh: Edinburgh University Press, 2015.
Waas, B & Heerma van Voss, G. (eds), *Restatement of Labour Law in Europe Vol I: The Concept of Employee*, Oxford: Hart Publishing, 2017.

Journal Articles

Bruton, C. & O'Mahoney, S. 'Religious Discrimination and Expression of Religion: Manifestation of Religious Beliefs in the Workplace', *Irish Employment Law Journal* 10(2) (2013): 46.
Buckley, L. 'Can the Criminal Law Put an End to the "Cover-Up" of Clerical Sexual Abuse?', *Irish Criminal Law Journal* 24(4) (2014): 98.
Burke-Murphy, E. 'Affidavits Must Be Administered on Religious Text', *Irish Law Times* 34 (2016): 126.
Coakley, J. 'Religion, National Identity and Political Change in Modern Ireland', *Irish Political Studies* 17(1) (2002): 4.
Coen, M. 'Religious Ethos and Employment Equality: A Comparative Irish Perspective', *Legal Studies,* 28(3) (2008): 452.
Cowley, C. 'Conscientious Objection in Healthcare and the Duty to Refer', *Journal of Medical Ethics* 43(4) (2017): 207.
Cryan, A. 'Changing Demographics: Legal Responses to Polygamy and the Challenges Ahead for Ireland', *Irish Journal of Family Law* 19(4) (2016): 82.
Daly, E. 'Re-evaluating the Purpose of Church-State Separation in the Irish Constitution: The Endowment Clause as a Protection of Religious Freedom and Equality', *Judicial Studies Institute Journal* 2 (2008): 86.

Doe, N. 'Towards a "Common Law" on Religion in the European Union', *Journal of Religion, State and Society* 37 (2009): 147.

Donnelly, S. & Inglis, T. 'The Media and the Catholic Church in Ireland: Reporting Clerical Child Sex Abuse', *Journal of Contemporary Religion* 25(1) (2010): 1–19.

Enright, M. '"Preferring the Stranger?" Towards an Irish Approach to Muslim Divorce Practice', *Irish Jurist* 49(1) (2013): 65.

Enright, M. 'Whither White Western Values? Comparative Perspectives on Culturally Motivated Decision-making for the Child', *Hibernian Law Journal* 7(1) (2007): 1.

Finlay, H.A. 'Farewell to Affinity and the Calculus of Kinship', *University of Tasmania Law Review* 5(1) (1975): 16.

Finegan, T. 'Conscientious Objection to Referrals', *Journal of Medical Ethics* 45(4) (2019): 277.

Forde, B. 'Church of Ireland Clergy and Employment Law', *Law & Justice – The Christian Law Review* 178 (2017): 80.

Fuller, L. 'Religion, Politics and Socio-Cultural Change in Twentieth Century Ireland', *The European Legacy* 10(1) (2005): 41.

Harding, M. 'The Curious Incident of the Marriage Act (no 2) 1537 and the Irish Statute Book', *Legal Studies* 32(1) (2012): 78.

Hogan, C. 'Accommodating Islam in the Denomination Irish Education System', *Journal of Muslim Minority Affairs* 31(4) (2011): 554.

Hogan, C. 'Accommodation of Faith in the Irish Workplace: European and Irish Perspectives', *Irish Employment Law Journal* 14(2) (2017): 37.

Hogan, G.W. 'Law and Religion: Church-State Relations in Ireland from Independence to the Present Day', *The American Journal of Comparative Law* 35(1) (1987): 47.

Hogan, G. 'De Valera, the Constitution and the Historians', *Irish Jurist* 40 (2005): 291.

Kamal, J. 'Justified Interference with Religious Freedom: The European Court of Human Rights and the Need for Mediating Doctrine under Article 9(2)', *Columbia Journal of Transnational Law* 46 (2008): 667.

Keating, A. 'The Uses and Abuses of Censorship: God, Ireland and the Battle to Extend Censorship Post 1929', *Estudios Irlandes* 9 (2014): 67.

Keating, A. 'Censorship the Cornerstone of Catholic Ireland', *Journal of Church and State* 57(2) (2015): 289.

Keogh, D. 'The Irish Constitutional Revolution: An Analysis of the Making of the Constitution', *Administration* 35 (1985): 4.

Leahy, S. & O'Sullivan, K. 'Changing Conceptions of Marriage in Ireland: Law and Practice', *Child and Family Law Quarterly* 30(3) (2018): 279.

Leahy, S. 'Criminal Offences Relating to Marriage formation: Reflections on Recent Developments', *Irish Journal of Family Law* 22(4) (2019): 87.

Mawhinney, A. 'Freedom of Religion in the Irish Primary School System: A Failure to Protect Human Rights?', *Legal Studies* 27(3) (2007): 379.

Mawhinney, A. 'A Discriminating Education System: Religious Admission Policies in Irish Schools and International Human Rights Law', *International Journal of Children's Rights* 20(4) (2012): 603.

McCormack-George, D.A.J.L. 'Sacerdotal Privilege in Irish Law', *Irish Law Times* 33(7) (2015): 104.

McGowan, D. 'Governed by Marriage Law', *Social and Legal Studies* 25(3) (2016): 311.

McLoughlin, J. '"In the presence of Almighty God" – The Human Rights Violations at the Heart of the Irish Constitution', *Irish Law Times* 35(17) (2017): 230.

McMahon, B. '"*People v. Philips*" in Light of Contemporary Developments in Ireland and the U. S.', *American Journal of Irish Studies* 11 (2014): 89.

Mee, J. 'Marriage Partnership and the Prohibited Degrees of Relationship', *Irish Law Times* 27 (2009): 259.

Mullally, S. and O'Donovan, D. 'Religion and Ireland's "Public Squares": Education, the Family and Expanding Equality Claims', *Public Law* (April) (2011): 284.

Ní Shuilleabháin, M. 'Marriage, Divorce and Stagnation in the Irish Conflict of Laws', *Irish Jurist* 52(2) (2014): 68.

Ní Shuilleabháin, M. 'Foreign Divorce Recognition and Residence: A Critical Analysis of H v H', *Irish Jurist* 57 (2017): 162.

Nussbaum, M. 'A Right to Marry?', *California Law Review* 98(3) (2010): 667.

O'Higgins, P. 'Blasphemy in Irish Law', *Modern Law Review* 23 (1960): 151.

O'Sullivan, K. 'The Legacy Continues: Ancillary Relief on Divorce in Ireland', *Journal of Family Studies* 25(3) (2019): 337.

O'Sullivan, K. 'Access to Marriage: Consanguinity and Affinity Prohibitions in National and International Context', *Irish Journal of Family Law* 22(2) (2019): 8.

O'Sullivan, K. 'Location, Location, Location: The Future of Weddings Law in Ireland and England' *Journal of Social Welfare and Family Law* 43(3) (2021): (forthcoming).

Pearson, M. 'Article 9 at a Crossroads: Interference Before and After Eweida', *Human Rights Law Review* 13(3) (2013): 580.

Reid, C. 'Nothing But the Truth', *Law Society Gazette* (May) (2016): 34.

Sandberg, R. 'Church-State Relations in Europe: From Legal Models to an Interdisciplinary Approach', *Journal of Religion in Europe* 1(3) (2008): 329.

Scharbrodt, O. 'Muslim Immigration to the Republic of Ireland: Trajectories and Dynamics since World War II', *Éire-Ireland* 47(1) (2012): 221.

Staunton, C. '"It's about Actually Having a Proactive Regulatory Framework Versus a Reactive One": Stakeholder Perspectives on the Governance of Embryonic Stem Cell Research in Ireland', *Medico-Legal Journal of Ireland* 24(2) (2018): 97.

Tobin, B. 'Marriage Equality in Ireland: The Politico-Legal Context', *International Journal of Law, Policy and the Family* 30(2) (2016): 115.

Todd Parker, M. 'The Freedom to Manifest Religious Belief: An Analysis of the Necessity Clauses of the ICCPR and the ECHR', *Duke Journal of Comparative & International Law* 17 (2006): 91.

Walsh, W.J. 'The Priest-Penitent Privilege: An Hibernocentric Essay in Postcolonial Jurisprudence', *Indiana Law Journal* 80 (2005): 1037.

Ward, P. 'The Path to Divorce', *Irish Law Times* 12 (1994): 29.

Index

The numbers here refer to paragraph numbers.

Index

www.ingramcontent.com/pod-product-compliance
Lightning Source LLC
Chambersburg PA
CBHW071343230926
51846CB00002B/435

* 9 7 8 9 4 0 3 5 1 7 2 8 5 *